After early experience with J.C. Williamson's, Sydney University Dramatic Society (SUDS), Nimrod Theatre and Melbourne Theatre Company, Nick Enright trained for the theatre at New York University School of the Arts, where he studied playwriting with Israel Horovitz.

His plays include *On the Wallaby, Daylight Saving, St James Infirmary, Mongrels, A Property of the Clan, The Quartet From Rigoletto, Blackrock, Good Works, Playgrounds, Spurboard, Chasing the Dragon* and *A Poor Student*. With Justin Monjo, he adapted Tim Winton's *Cloudstreet* for the stage.

For film Nick wrote *Lorenzo's Oil* with George Miller (for which they were nominated for Academy and WGA Awards for Best Original Screenplay), and *Blackrock*; and for television *Coral Island* and the miniseries *Come In Spinner*. Many of his plays have been broadcast and he has also written original work for radio.

With composer Terence Clarke, he wrote the musicals *The Venetian Twins* and *Summer Rain*. Other musical collaborations include *Miracle City* with Max Lambert, *Mary Bryant* and *The Good Fight* with David King and the book for the Australian production of *The Boy From Oz*.

Good Works and *Cloudstreet* won Melbourne Green Room Awards for Best Play. *Daylight Saving, A Property of the Clan, Blackrock* (screenplay) and *Cloudstreet* have all won Writers' Guild Gold AWGIE Awards. Nick was honoured to receive the 1998 Sidney Myer Performing Arts Award.

Nick had long been involved as a teacher and writer with young actors, especially at the National Institute of Dramatic Art (NIDA) and the Western Australian Academy of Performing Arts (WAAPA), as well as community-based companies such as Freewheels. He was recently instrumental in setting up, with Jessica Machin and Julian Louis, State of Play, an actors' ensemble in Sydney which develops and presents new works.

Nick Enright died in Sydney in March 2003.

Steve Bisley as Gerry in the 2002 Sydney Theatre Company production.
(Photo: Heidrun Löhr)

Nick Enright

A MAN
WITH FIVE
CHILDREN

Currency Press
Sydney

CURRENCY PLAYS

First published in 2003
by Currency Press Pty Ltd,
Gadigal Land, Suite 310, 46–56 Kippax Street, Surry Hills, NSW 2010, Australia
enquiries@currency.com.au
www.currency.com.au

NATIONAL LIBRARY OF AUSTRALIA CIP DATA

Enright, Nicholas, 1950–2003.
A man with five children.
ISBN 0 86819 691 6.
1. Fatherhood–Drama. 2. Child development–Drama. I. Title.
A822.3

Publication of this title was assisted by the Commonwealth Government through the Australia Council, its arts funding and advisory body.

Set by Dean Nottle
Cover design by Kate Florance, Currency Press
Front cover photo shows Steve Bisley as Gerry in the 2002 Sydney Theatre Company production of *A Man with Five Children*. Back cover photo shows Justine Clarke as Annie, Travis McMahon as Cam and Steve Bisley as Gerry in the same production. (Photos: Heidrun Löhr)

For George Miller and George Ogilvie with thanks and love.

Contents

Currency Press acknowledges the Traditional Owners of the Country on which we live and work. We pay our respects to all Aboriginal and Torres Strait Islander Elders, past and present.

On screens in background (from left): Kenneth Moraleda as Roger and Genevieve O'Reilly as Susannah; in foreground (from left): Margaret Harvey as Jessie, Steve Bisley as Gerry, Travis McMahon as Cam and Justine Clarke as Annie in the 2002 Sydney Theatre Company production. (Photo: Heidrun Löhr)

The Man Behind the Camera

John McCallum

There is a scene in Dennis O'Rourke's 1991 film *The Good Woman of Bangkok* in which he keeps the camera running on the young woman who is his subject as she asks him to stop. She is Aoi, a Thai prostitute, and O'Rourke's starting point for making his movie about her was that he would first be a client. It is a confronting scene not only because of this, and because he kept shooting, but also because he put it into the final cut. He had a relationship with her, and the emotions and needs of each of them are as much a part of the film as are the 'documentary' details of her life and world. O'Rourke said later:

> In *The Good Woman of Bangkok*, by deliberate acts of transgression and exposure, both fictional and real, I contrived to... collapse the insulating critical distance which normally exists between the documentary film maker and his/her audience.[1]

The film controversially challenged the central principle of the old notion of documentary—the objectivity of the filmmaker—a principle that Gerry in *A Man With Five Children* clings to desperately and increasingly unconvincingly, as he becomes more and more involved in the lives of his subjects, his five children.

A closer model for this play is Michael Apted's extraordinary series of films that began in 1964 with *7-Up*. In that year he took 14 children aged seven, chosen from all classes of English society, and filmed them talking about their lives and hopes. He has revisited them every seven years since, aged 14, 21, 28, 35 and 42, and documented what has

---

[1] 'Documentary Fictions: Bibliography, Truth and Moral Lies', Documenting a Life, a seminar at the National Library of Australia. 26 October 1996. See www.nla.gov.au/events/doclife/orourke.html.

happened to them, how their lives have changed and how they have reflected on their experiences—including the experience of becoming famous and having their past looming so publicly over them. Perhaps the series is not over yet. By the arithmetic, at least, *49-Up* is due out in two year's time.

One of the remarkable things in the Up series, apart from the fascinating opportunity to follow human lives over such a long period, is that the subjects keep agreeing to be part of it. A large international audience keeps checking up on how they are doing. There were still 11 of the original 14 participating in *42-Up* in 1998, 35 years after they were originally recruited.

Why do they keep agreeing to take part? They had no choice when they were seven, but from then on they were part of a project larger than themselves. They become increasingly reluctant, but Apted is clearly a persuasive, or perhaps manipulative director, or perhaps simply a friend to whom they owe something. They also become famous (although the point of the original project was supposed to be that they were ordinary) and perhaps they like that. As the series progresses their fame folds back into their lives, their partners become drawn into the process and they keep having to look back, not on their actual lives but on how those lives have been presented to the public.

One of the most popular of Apted's children has been the lonely Neil, a delightful, bright, young seven-year-old, who by 28 was all but homeless and by 35 was living a sad wreck of a life in the Shetlands. By 42 he had begun to get his life together again and audiences around the world responded to this development as if it were a scripted turning point in a dramatic fiction, which in effect it was, although perhaps not for him.

Part of the appeal of the Up series is the idea that it is somehow authentic, that its characters are 'real'. It's like the appeal of recent 'reality' television. We enjoy 'Big Brother' and 'Survivor' because its protagonists are supposed to be ordinary people like ourselves, although everything we know about the production of these shows and the hype that surrounds them screams artifice and construction.

Nick Enright's fine play conflates Apted's project and dramatises these issues. At the opening his character Gerry talks directly to the audience. He asks permission to film his chosen children from age seven and to screen his edited version of their lives each year on national television until they turn 21. In the second act, having become involved with their lives as more than a filmmaker, he asks them to agree to an extension of the project. It becomes clear that he has become so involved that he wants to keep filming them until he dies, or they do. This is partly because the 'story' is so good, including for his career, but partly also because by now he can't let go of them. He has allowed one of them to move into his house, he has had sex with another, he has betrayed a third and he has fallen in love with a fourth, but he still keeps up his pretence of objectivity until the very end of the play, when suddenly the camera is turned back on him, and he is forced to speak to it, as he has made them speak to his camera for the last 28 years.

Gerry says at the opening, 'You know the old maxim? "Give me a child at seven, I'll show you the adult." I say, give me a child at seven and let's see where he goes, where she goes.' And so he acquires his children and his recording of their lives becomes an intervention that turns out to be a major influence on where they go. It's like the Heisenberg principle in physics or the O'Rourke principle in documentary filmmaking—the observer is as much a part of the phenomenon as is the observed. The only way you can know what is happening is to watch, but the act of watching collapses the indeterminacy about what is happening and creates its own reality. How can Gerry possibly know, let alone document, what these lives might have been like had he not been there recording them?

The big difference between Enright's stage play and Apted's television series is, of course, that the real observer/manipulator in *A Man With Five Children* is not Gerry but Enright. He is an author in a way that Apted is not. His play is a fiction, he has honestly invented these people and his telling of their stories is highly affecting. The equivalent of Neil is Roger, the gifted and privileged boy whose life suddenly falls apart and whom Gerry casts out, telling him to make his own way, but who keeps coming back to haunt him. Susannah's thwarted poetic impulse is crippled by her love for Gerry and his inadequate response to it. He supports and encourages Jessie because he loves her and, in an embarrassing scene, he suddenly reinterprets that love as romantic rather than parental, because his relationship with his 'children' is based in his illusion that he has no responsibility for them. His relationship with Cam becomes destructive—a kind of mid-life crisis for a man who has only ever looked at life through a lens.

By the end of the play Gerry has become the classic absent father who only does 'quality time' with his children and is seldom there when they really need him. He keeps editing himself out of the interviews and by the end he seems to have edited himself out of his own life. Or perhaps he is tentatively beginning to creep back into it, as something more than the man behind the camera.

Sydney
March 2003

Playwright's Note

Nick Enright

This play began life as a student exercise at the Western Australian Academy of Performing Arts in May 1998, when Peter Kingston, head of the theatre course, invited me to devise a workshop piece with a group of third-year actors whom I knew well after working with them in the first two years of their training.

I had been fascinated for years by documentary films (of which the most notable and I think the first is the Apted *Seven Up* series) which chronicle the lives, growth and development of a group of young people from early childhood. My first impulse was to investigate the off-camera lives of such a group as they brace themselves for another interview. But as the piece developed, it declared its true subject, the film-maker.

The WAAPA show, a four-hour epic called *Five Sevens*, never really came to grips with this elusive character; but in two subsequent workshops at STC, under the astute guidance of David Berthold and Marion Potts, we began to reshape the material from the point of view of a childless man who, unlike Michael Apted and his imitators, chooses a small group of subjects, and charts their lives from year to year, showing his latest episode of *Five Children* on Australian television every New Year's Day; a kind of national soap-opera-verite, if you like. Jeremy Sims, one of the many good minds who worked on the material, articulated the hardest question: is it about the man or the children? He and his colleagues made me see that simply to chronicle five lives over several decades is to attempt to do on stage what video does far better; but if the film-maker is the subject, then the play can try to examine not the process of such films, but their rationale, and the dangers they present not only for their participants—and audiences—but for their creator.

Though the play has been substantially rewritten since the Perth workshop, it could never have come into being without the support of the WAAPA staff and administration, and the creative contribution of the Academy graduating students: my co-director Kim Hardwick, stage manager Heather Dransfield, and actors David Bishop, Deborah Clay, Ditch Davey, Jodie Duncan, Astrid Garton, Jonathan Gavin, Susan Godfrey, Thomas Holesgrove, Hayley McElhinney, Matthew Moore, Kingsley Reeve, Jane Ruggiero, Kristian Schmidt, Blair Venn and Nicole Winkler. My thanks to them all.

Thanks too, to the Sydney Theatre Company for generously affording me two workshops (as well as several readings) as part of the play's continuing development, and then for taking on the play's technological demands in a full production with the splendid group of artists who are named opposite. Under George Ogilvie's astute and sensitive guidance, I believe all of us enjoyed one of the richest collaborations of our working lives; certainly that was so for me.

Sydney
November 2002

A Man with Five Children was first produced by Sydney Theatre Company at the Wharf One Theatre, Sydney, on 9 January 2002, with the following cast:

GERRY	Steve Bisley
ROGER	Kenneth Moraleda
JESSIE	Margaret Harvey
CAM	Travis McMahon
SUSANNAH	Genevieve O'Reilly
ZOE	Kate Mulvany
DOUG	Anthony Weigh
ANNIE	Justine Clarke
THEO	Arky Michael

Director, George Ogilvie
Set Designer, Stephen Curtis
Costume Designer, Anna French
Lighting Designer, Rory Dempster
Sound Designer, Sam Petty
Composer, Alan John
Assistant Director, Michael Bates

CHARACTERS

GERRY

ROGER

JESSIE

CAM

SUSANNAH

ZOE

DOUG

ANNIE

THEO

SETTING

The action of the play takes place in and around Sydney and Melbourne in the years 1972–2000.

A NOTE ON THE TEXT

The stage directions mark the distinction between the stage action and the film sequences. In the original production, the 'on screen' sequences of childhood and early adolescence were played live on the stage accompanied by graphics and still photographs on a screen which surmounted the playing area. From the sequence with Roger at 17, all interviews played on screen.

ACT ONE

SCENE ONE: 1972

A bare stage. GERRY 28 *approaches the audience.*

GERRY: I want your child, and yours, and yours. What do I want from them? One day out of their lives. One day a year, till they turn twenty-one. One day for the camera to follow them. To a football game, a ballet class, a birthday party. One day a year for them to speak and be heard. Which day? You say. Or I say. Or maybe they say. You've all seen some of my films. Now you know the way Gerard Hilferty works. I get close, and I stay close. I'll try to not to bring along any preconceptions. I'll try to bring nothing but a camera and a microphone. You know that old maxim? 'Give me a child at seven, I'll show you the adult.' I don't buy that. I say, give me a child at seven and let's see where he goes, where she goes. No money will change hands. You'll have a record of your child's life. Your children will have a way to chart their own lives. And once a year, New Year's Day, on national television, we'll show some moments from the year these children have lived, from the day they give me. I want your child, yours, yours, yours, yours. Five children to speak for young Australia. I hope all five will want to come with me on the journey. And if they do, we'll meet at the gates of the zoo.

He waits. ROGER *appears.*

G'day.

ROGER: My name is Roger Chan.

GERRY: I'm Gerry.

ROGER: My father told me what you're going to do. You talk to us. Then you do it again next year. And you'll put the two films together and see how we've changed.

GERRY: That's pretty right.

ROGER: And then the next year, you'll do the same thing. But why?

JESSIE *approaches.*

JESSIE: Why are we here? Zoos are bad places.

GERRY: We could talk about that. You're Jessie. I'm Gerry. This is Roger.

He sees CAM *approaching.*

Hi.

CAM: I'm hungry.

GERRY: We'll have lunch at the zoo.

CAM: I'm hungry now.

GERRY: Jessie, Roger. This is Cam.

ROGER: Cam? Is that short for something?

CAM: Cameron. Duhh.

SUSANNAH 7 *approaches.* ZOE 7 *trails her.*

SUSANNAH: She won't say her name. Are all these children seven? She
   seems quite young for seven. I'm seven. I'm tall for my age.

GERRY: Susannah, this is Jessie—

JESSIE: Hi.

GERRY: Cam.

ROGER: Roger. Roger Chan.

JESSIE: What's your name?

ZOE: Zoe.

SUSANNAH: She wouldn't tell me.

GERRY: Zoe. Jessie. Cam. Susannah. Roger. You'll want to practise those
   names.

ROGER: Zoe. Cam. Jessie. Susannah. Roger. I know them.

GERRY: Let's go to the zoo. You walk ahead. I'll follow.

He picks up the camera.

CAM: I don't want to.

ROGER: We'll see ourselves on television.

CAM: I don't fucken want to.

ROGER *starts to play with a high-tech game.*

SUSANNAH: He's rude. He shouldn't be here.

CAM: You shouldn't. You talk funny. She shouldn't. She's an abo. I hate
   abos.

JESSIE: Why?

CAM: Australia for Australians. [*To* JESSIE] Bloody abo boong. [*To* ROGER] And you. Slope-features.

GERRY: Hey! I don't want any name-calling. Never again. You're all different. You're all Australians. I want you all to respect one another. And I want you all to stay. Every one of you.

　　CAM *is walking away.*

Specially you, Cam.

CAM: What'll you give me?

ROGER: Didn't you hear? No money will change hands.

　　CAM *grabs for the game.* ROGER *won't let go.*

CAM: Get me one of them?

GERRY: No. I can't give you anything. But maybe we can do something together.

From left: Steve Bisley as Gerry, Kenneth Moraleda as Roger and Travis McMahon as Cam in the 2002 Sydney Theatre Company production. (Photo: Heidrun Löhr)

CAM: Take me to the footie?

GERRY: The footie? I reckon I could do that. If I can bring my camera.

CAM: All right. When?

GERRY: Some time this season.

ROGER: Can I come too?

GERRY: Sure.

CAM: I'm good at footie. See?

> *He grabs* ROGER*'s game and goes to dropkick it.*

ROGER: Don't!

> CAM *throws it into the air.* ROGER *catches it.* CAM *runs off, followed by* ROGER. GERRY *films.*

SUSANNAH: I like Gerry. Do you like him? Zoe?

ZOE: I don't know. [*To* JESSIE] Do you?

JESSIE: When he came to our school he hid behind the trees. [*To* GERRY] Didn't you?

GERRY: I wasn't hiding. I was looking.

JESSIE: Looking for what?

GERRY: A girl with a purple hair ribbon.

JESSIE: Purple is my favourite colour.

SUSANNAH: I like pink.

> *She goes off chattering to* GERRY.

SUSANNAH 7: [*on screen*] My name is Susannah. I'm seven years old. In French you don't quite say that, you say 'I have seven years'. My daddy's French. He's a neurosurgeon. He does operations with a thing like a magnifying glass, and he can see every tiny little part of someone's brain. I want to be a doctor too. I want to look after sick people. And I'd like a turtle and a yellow parrot… yes, like the ones we saw today, and I want lots of friends to come and play, and… Thank you for the lunch, it was very nice.

JESSIE 7: [*on screen*] I've got a swing in our backyard, my dad made it, and I swing really high and my mum says, Jessie I can see your purple undies! I love purple, I've got a purple hair ribbon, see?

CAM 7: [*on screen*] I want to see my dad. He's a soldier. He drives a tank. Yeah… and, and he's a security guard sometimes.

ROGER 7: [*on screen*] My father drives a Mercedes 230SL. It's silver. He's an engineer. He's from Malaysia. My mother's Filipino. Two sisters. We were all born here. We're Australians.

ZOE 7: [*on screen*] I don't know what I want to be.

SUSANNAH 7: [*on screen*] I can sing songs in French. I'd like to be a doctor and a singer. And a mother with a baby. A girl. Boys are silly. I know this song. It's my favourite.

　　She sings.

'*Au clair de la lune, mon ami Pierrot,*
Prête-moi ta plume pour écrire un mot.
Ma chandelle est morte, je n'ai plus de feu.
Ouvre-moi ta porte, pour l'amour de Dieu.'

◆ ◆ ◆ ◆ ◆

Genevieve O'Reilly (left) as Susannah and Margaret Harvey as Jessie in the 2002 Sydney Theatre Company production. (Photo: Heidrun Löhr)

SCENE TWO: 1975

A state children's home. As SUSANNAH *sings,* CAM 10 *plays alone.*

GERRY: You're pretty brave. You don't have to be. You're going to miss her.

CAM: She's better off dead. That's what the ambos said.

GERRY: I bet you'll like your uncle and auntie.

CAM: I never seen them.

GERRY: They're coming for you today.

CAM: Why can't I live with you?

GERRY: Hey. I'm really flattered.

CAM: What does that mean?

GERRY: It's a nice thing to hear. Your uncle and aunt have kids. You'll have cousins to play with.

CAM: I want to go with you.

GERRY: You'd have no mum. I don't have a wife or a girlfriend.

CAM: Get one.

GERRY: I'll take you to the footie again next season. Now I have a plane to catch. I've got your new address. I'll send you a postcard. Give us a hug?

    CAM *resists, then hugs him fiercely.*

◆ ◆ ◆ ◆ ◆

SCENE THREE: 1977

ROGER 12 *plays with a figure of Obi Wan Kenobe.*

ROGER: 'I understand you've become a good pilot yourself. Your father wanted you to have this when you were old enough.' 'What is it?' 'Your father's light sabre. An elegant weapon. May the force be with you.'

◆ ◆ ◆ ◆ ◆

SCENE FOUR: 1978

ZOE *and* JESSIE *at 13.*

ZOE: My mum's got a new boyfriend.

JESSIE: Do they do it in your house?

ZOE: I don't know!

JESSIE: I bet you listen.

ZOE: No!

JESSIE: Yes.

ZOE: Yes. Have you got a boyfriend?

JESSIE: No. I pashed a guy on a school camp.

ZOE: I've never kissed anyone.

      JESSIE *kisses* ZOE *lightly on the lips.*

JESSIE: Now you have.

ZOE: You're a good kisser.

      She kisses JESSIE. *They see* GERRY *is shooting them.*

JESSIE: One day someone'll sneak up on you, Gerry. And you won't know where to look.

◆ ◆ ◆ ◆ ◆

SCENE FIVE: 1978

SUSANNAH 13 *shows the results of a science experiment for the camera: a dissected frog, whose brain and spinal chord she displays.*

SUSANNAH: The frog has a highly developed nervous system. See? Brain, spinal chord and nerves. You can't see the nerves. The important parts of a frog's brain are a bit like parts of the human brain, but the frog has a very small cerebrum. Humans have a very large cerebrum, which is the centre of many important life processes. Well... like emotions and... language, and... poetry. Frogs aren't supposed to have feelings. I'm not sure about that. Do you think this one knew it was going to die? How do you think it felt?

◆ ◆ ◆ ◆ ◆

SCENE SIX: 1979

1979. Jessie's house. JESSIE 14 *reads from a piece of paper.*

JESSIE: 'Last year the US government spent over a hundred billion dollars on nuclear weapons and a further thirty billion on maintaining and expanding its chain of bases and tracking systems. The Soviet government spent…'

　　　GERRY *is shaking his head.*

You said, make it simple. This is simple.

GERRY: People can read facts in a newspaper. You want to stir them, move them—

JESSIE: Who'll get moved by a fourteen-year-old?

GERRY: Other fourteen-year-olds. Fifteen, sixteen, seventeen-year-olds, anyone. Tell them what you feel.

JESSIE: What I feel. What I feel is why am I doing this?

GERRY: Maybe because we don't want the world to blow itself up?

JESSIE: Good one, Gerry. I mean why me?

GERRY: Why not you? You've got strong ideas.

JESSIE: You just heard them.

　　　He takes her speech from her.

GERRY: You've got your experience. Say what you enjoy about life. How you want to go on enjoying it. What peace means to young Australia.

JESSIE: Young Australia?

GERRY: Young black Australia.

JESSIE: I'm just Jessie.

GERRY: What does Jessie want from life?

JESSIE: I won't talk that talk in front of strangers.

GERRY: Forget them. Do it for your mum and dad.

JESSIE: They'll be marching. I want to march with them.

GERRY: You get up and speak on Sunday, you'll make them proud of you.

JESSIE: It might change me.

GERRY: Jessie, when your mother speaks for your mob, people listen, don't they? When your dad marches, blokes march with him, yeah? You're her daughter, and his. All through your life, people will be drawn to you. They'll want to listen. That's a great gift. Why not accept it?

JESSIE: All right. I'll do it.

GERRY: Good on you.

JESSIE: But I won't let you film it.

JESSIE's *voice resounds as though outdoors.*

JESSIE'S VOICE: My name is Jessie. I'm fourteen. I want to be fifteen. Then sixteen. I want time to be all the things that I can be. None of us want that time taken from us. We want our chance at life.

◆ ◆ ◆ ◆ ◆

Steve Bisley (left background) as Gerry and Margaret Harvey as Jessie in the 2002 Sydney Theatre Company production. (Photo: Heidrun Löhr)

SCENES SEVEN / EIGHT: 1979

ZOE *and* SUSANNAH 14 *hear this speech in separate spaces.*

GERRY: 'I want time to be all the things that I can be.' She wrote that. And then she said it. To a hundred thousand people in the Domain. [*To* ZOE] Did you know about it?

> ZOE *nods.*

And you weren't there? Jessie's a good friend, isn't she?

ZOE: She's all right.

SUSANNAH: I could never do that, stand up and speak like that. We marched, of course. Jessie was very good. Didn't you think so?

GERRY: She was great, Zoe. Want to hear the rest?

ZOE: No.

SUSANNAH: My father said you chose her for passion. And me because…

GERRY: And you because… Why you? Susannah?

SUSANNAH: Because I'm intelligent. And observant.

GERRY: Do you think that's true?

SUSANNAH: You'd be more able to answer that.

GERRY: Do you want to do this another time?

ZOE: Might as well get it over with.

GERRY: Is that how you feel? You can say that. You can say anything, about anything. Let's start with school.

ZOE: Where we always start.

SUSANNAH: Yes I do, I do want to do well.

GERRY: What, to please your parents?

SUSANNAH: No, not to please my parents, but because I have standards.

ZOE: The teachers know who's going to do well. They get the attention, but the rest of us… I want to find a job.

GERRY: What kind of job?

ZOE: A job. Any job.

GERRY: Is that what you really want?

ZOE: I really want to stop answering questions.

GERRY: You don't like this process?

ZOE *shrugs.*

What do you think of it? Come on.

ZOE: I look at Jessie and them, and I think… you really want to know?
I think I'm the one who's ordinary.

GERRY: And ordinary means…?

ZOE: Ordinary means the one who's not going anywhere.

SUSANNAH: I think observant is a good thing to be. You're observing us,
aren't you? And I watch you, I watch a lot of people. I try to work
out what people are thinking. And feeling.

GERRY: Do you ever write about that?

SUSANNAH: Write? No. I don't write.

ZOE: You're weird. You've got weird eyes. X-ray vision.

GERRY: You don't write?

SUSANNAH: No. Yes, I write poetry. How did you know that?

GERRY: Do you ever show anyone?

SUSANNAH: No. No, it's too… It's too… Can we stop this now?

GERRY: You can stop any time.

◆ ◆ ◆ ◆ ◆

SCENE NINE: 1980

The final credit roll of the 1980 edition of 'Five Children'…

CAM 7: [*on screen*] My dad's real strong. Me? I'm fast. Want to see me
run?

ROGER 7: [*on screen*] I was born on January 26th, 1965. That's Australia
Day.

SUSANNAH 7: [*on screen*] I still want to be a doctor and a singer. And be
a mother with a baby.

ZOE 7: [*on screen*] I still don't know what I want to be.

JESSIE 8: [*on screen*] The girls at school, we do dancing but we don't let
the boys see, we do it under the trees, under the trees is girls only
and we chase them away if they come near. Boys' germs!

CAM 8: [*on screen*] Carn, Wests! Carn, Wests!

ROGER 9: [*on screen*] I'd like to be a pilot. I don't mind, but in a very fast plane. My father's going to buy a plane. He's got three cars. I like planes. I like cars better.

ZOE 9: [*on screen*] Zoe Watson, pay attention, pay attention Zoe, you're not paying attention, you're such a naughty girl, how will you learn if you don't…

CAM 10: [*on screen*] Carn, Wests! Carn, Wests! Hit him, Boydie! Hit him!

ROGER 10: [*on screen*] An engineer. Like my dad. He's building the new aquarium for the zoo.

ZOE 11: [*on screen*] It's like a story, but with dancing. This girl turned into a swan. Or was she a swan who turned into a girl? I wouldn't know, I just got taken.

ROGER 11: [*on screen*] I say I'm an Australian, just like you. I was born on Australia Day.

CAM 12: [*on screen*] I live with my uncle Kevin and them. They took me when my mum died. They don't like me that much. I don't like them that much.

ZOE 13: [*on screen, to* JESSIE] Have you got a boyfriend?

JESSIE 13: [*on screen*] No. I pashed a guy on a school camp.

ZOE 13: [*on screen*] I've never kissed anyone.

JESSIE *kisses* ZOE *lightly on the lips.*

JESSIE 13: [*on screen*] Now you have.

ZOE 13: [*on screen*] You're a good kisser.

She kisses JESSIE.

SUSANNAH 13: [*on screen*] I think TV is stupid. I like reading. Great novels. *Wuthering Heights,* that's my favourite. My father says novels are a waste of time because they're not true. Do you think that?

ROGER 14: [*on screen*] A pilot? Did I say that? And an engineer! You need to be heaps better at maths than I ever will be. I wouldn't mind being a pilot. What I want most? I want to design pinball machines. I want to own a pinball place. No, really, what I want most is a Maserati.

CAM 14: [*on screen*] You know what I reckon? I must be missing something. Like an engine part, sort of. A bit got left out.

ZOE 14: [*on screen*] I think I'm the one who's ordinary. Ordinary means the one who's not going anywhere.

SUSANNAH 14: [*on screen*] If I am observant, I think observant is a good thing to be. I try to work out what people are thinking. And feeling. Write? No. I don't write. Yes, I write poetry. No. No, it's too… Can we stop this now?

A TV news grab: JESSIE *at the anti-nuclear rally.*

JESSIE 14: [*on screen*] I want time to be all the things that I can be. None of us want that time taken from us. We want our chance at life.

Cheering and applause from an unseen crowd.

❖ ❖ ❖ ❖ ❖

SCENE TEN: 1980

THE FIVE CHILDREN 15, *watch themselves on screen.*

SUSANNAH: I like it.

ZOE: I hate that kiss.

GERRY: The kiss was in last year.

JESSIE: So why show it again?

GERRY: That's how I build a rhythm.

JESSIE: You said you wouldn't show my speech.

GERRY: I said I wouldn't shoot it. That was ABC news footage.

JESSIE: But when you put it in here—

SUSANNAH: You look fantastic. I'm proud to know you.

JESSIE: Is everyone else happy? Roger?

ROGER: I don't have a problem.

JESSIE: Even if he makes you look…

Silence.

ROGER: What?

GERRY: Jess, that speech happened, in front of a hundred thousand strangers. I don't create your lives. I follow them.

JESSIE: Where? How far?

GERRY: Till you're twenty-one, I hope. That was the deal.

JESSIE: With our mums and dads, when we were seven. Now we're about to be sixteen. Old enough to leave school, leave home—

GERRY: Why are you speaking for everyone?

JESSIE: Fair enough. Someone else.

> *Silence.*

Cam, what do you reckon?

CAM: About what?

JESSIE: What you just saw.

CAM: Heap of bullshit.

GERRY: What's bullshit?

CAM: All of it. [JESSIE] Her wanking on. [ROGER] Him, saying he's Australian.

ROGER: I am Australian, same as you.

CAM: Fuck off. Look at yourself.

ROGER: Are you stupid, or what?

GERRY: Boys—

CAM: Don't you call me stupid—

GERRY: Let it go.

CAM: I'll punch your fucken head in, all right?

> *He shoves at* ROGER, *who shoves back.*

Fucken slit-eye, fucken slope. You want a go?

GERRY: No! Apologise, Cam.

CAM: No way.

> *He goes.*

GERRY: He can't go far, I'm driving him home. Roger, I'm sorry—

ROGER: I am an Australian.

GERRY: Yes, mate.

ROGER: Why did you bring us together?

SUSANNAH: I enjoy seeing everyone. I like to feel that we belong. Don't you feel that? Zoe?

ZOE: How do you mean? Belong?

SUSANNAH: Like a kind of family.

JESSIE: This isn't a family. It's a game we got into before we knew the rules.

GERRY: We can make some rules. But did you hear Susannah? She likes to feel that we belong. There are young people watching you. Your stories tell them they're not alone, they see someone else growing up with the same needs, the same fears. There's someone out there that you speak to, each of you in your own way…

ZOE: As if.

> GERRY *catches* ZOE *making a face.*

GERRY: … even by not speaking. Think what you're doing for them. And stay on this journey, just a bit longer.

JESSIE: Just a bit longer. Okay. I'll give Dad a hand with the barbecue.

SUSANNAH: I'll help.

GERRY: Who'll go and find Cam? Zoe?

ZOE: Why? Okay…

> ZOE *goes.*

SUSANNAH: We are a family.

> *She follows* JESSIE *out.* ROGER *and* GERRY *are left alone.*

GERRY: Cam's not too happy. I think his uncle's pretty rough on him.

ROGER: Do you still take him to the football?

GERRY: We go sometimes. He plays now.

ROGER: Me too. I'm five-eight for the Sixteen Bs.

GERRY: Cam's into Aussie Rules now. He's good. He might make the Reserves next year.

ROGER: I don't follow Aussie Rules. I don't get it.

> ZOE *brings* CAM *in.*

GERRY: You blokes ready to shake hands?

> CAM *extends his hand.* ROGER *shakes it.*

Food's on. That way.

> ZOE *and* CAM *go.*

He plays rover. He's good. Fast.

ROGER: I'd like to see him.

GERRY: Come along one day.

ROGER: You said that years ago. You were going to take us both. Cam and me.

GERRY: Was I? Sorry, Roger. What do you think about him after what he said? Come on, put it to rest.

ROGER 15: [*on screen*] Cam's like a lot of people. They judge you by labels. I look Asian, I wear a private school uniform. So I'm not just a slope. I'm a rich slope, a rich smart slope who's meant to top the state in something.

CAM 15: [*on screen*] Roger? Roger's okay. I just want some of what he's got.

ROGER 7: [*on screen*] My father drives a Mercedes 230SL. It's silver. He's an engineer. He's from Malaysia. My mother's Filipino. Two sisters. We were all born here. We're Australians. We're building a new house. It's going to have a twenty-five-metre pool. I'm a good swimmer.

CAM 7: [*on screen*] You know my name. All right, my name's Cam. Short for Cameron, but no one calls me that. I want a bike, and a skateboard, and I want a car. Yeah, I can drive. I could work out how to.

◆ ◆ ◆ ◆ ◆

SCENE ELEVEN: 1981

GERRY *waits outside a suburban police station.* CAM 16 *emerges.*

GERRY: You fucked up big time, mate.

CAM: Yeah.

GERRY: Big big time.

CAM: I didn't hurt anybody. I just borrowed a car.

GERRY: Stole it, you mean.

CAM: I was bringing it back. Without a single fucken scratch on it.

GERRY: That was good luck. You're sixteen. You don't even have a licence. Come on, I'll drive you home.

CAM: Gerry… can we go somewhere, and talk?

GERRY: Mate. It's three a.m.

CAM: Look… could I crash at yours?

GERRY: Christ. Sure. Okay.

CAM: Just for a couple of weeks.

GERRY: A couple of weeks?

CAM: Would you let me… you know, stay with you…?

GERRY: Stay with me?

CAM: Just for a bit… just till I can—

GERRY: No, mate. How would your uncle and auntie take it?

CAM: They'd be glad to see the back of me. Please?

> *Silence.*

Fuck. Forget it.

GERRY: Where are you going?

CAM: What do you care?

> *He's going.*

GERRY: Cam. I'll do it. This is the deal. Listen up. You go back to training. You get off the speed, or whatever it is you're on. You find a job, and stick to it.

CAM: Okay.

GERRY: And you go back into the cop shop—

CAM: Eh?

GERRY: —and I shoot you coming out into the street.

CAM: No way. What happened tonight, that's my shit.

GERRY: So why did you call me?

CAM: We're mates. Aren't we?

GERRY: I tell your story. This is part of it.

CAM: No way.

GERRY: You want room and board? I've got the camera in the car. I'll knock it off and then I'll take you home.

> *Long silence.*

CAM: How do you want me?

GERRY: I don't want acting. Just you hitting the street.

◆ ◆ ◆ ◆ ◆

SCENE TWELVE: 1982

ROGER 17: [*on screen*] My father's given up expecting me to top the state in something. He'll be happy if I get into uni. I wouldn't mind. I like the idea of being a student. I don't know what I'd study…

◆ ◆ ◆ ◆ ◆

SCENE THIRTEEN: 1982

GERRY *finds* ZOE 17 *in a supermarket uniform. She's smoking.*

ZOE: I bet Jessie put you onto this.

GERRY: She told me you'd left school. She doesn't know you're working here.

ZOE: Two weeks.

GERRY: You've moved out.

ZOE: Mum was glad to see the back of me.

GERRY: You reckon?

ZOE: I'm in this great share house. Three guys in a band. I met them at the Zone.

GERRY: Big changes.

ZOE: First time anything's ever changed in my life.

GERRY: You're okay about leaving school?

ZOE: Why wouldn't I be?

GERRY: You want to talk about that?

ZOE: You want to talk about that.

GERRY: Not unless you do.

ZOE: You think I should have stayed.

GERRY: Can we shoot this?

ZOE: No. You do, don't you?

GERRY: If you finish school, you have options.

ZOE: You've got me mixed up with someone else.

GERRY: Who? [*Beat.*] Who do you mean? Jessie?

ZOE: Or Susannah. School can do something for girls like them. Doesn't mean shit to me.

GERRY: I've known you how long now? Ten years. More than half your life. Why do I think you're brighter than you do?

ZOE: Strangers stop me in the street. 'You're one of those five kids. You're the quiet one.' I say, no, I'm the dumb one.

GERRY: You don't. Do you?

> *She looks steadily at him.*

Don't let your life run away with you, okay?

ZOE: Why worry about me? We live our lives, you sit back and watch.

GERRY: I'd hate you to stuff yours up.

ZOE: Isn't that why you picked me?

GERRY: No, Zoe. I wanted to see where you'll go. I still want that.

ZOE: So why are you pushing me back to school?

GERRY: So you'll be able to make choices.

ZOE: I've made them. Now you back off.

GERRY: Does that mean you want to drop out of the project?

ZOE: Not yet. Those people in the street, they might as well get the whole story.

GERRY: Will you give it to them now?

ZOE: Now? I look like shit. Hang on...

> *As she takes a lipstick out... a grunge band plays.*

ZOE 17: [*on screen*] When the guys are playing at the Zone, I'm there. Working. I'm the door-bitch. I don't take shit from anyone. You'd be amazed. I'm rapt. I've made heaps of friends. It's like... my life just kicked in. Kicked in big time.

◆ ◆ ◆ ◆ ◆

SCENE FOURTEEN: DECEMBER 1983

The backyard of Susannah's house. GERRY *arrives with a gift and his camera.* SUSANNAH *sits on the ground meditating with a bound journal in her lap. He could shoot her without permission, but puts the camera down. She opens her eyes.*

SUSANNAH: Talk about transcendental. Your face was here… in my mind. And here you are.

GERRY: Your mum didn't tell me you were meditating.

SUSANNAH: She wouldn't know what meditation is.

GERRY: I just got back from Borneo.

SUSANNAH: Borneo. Your life…

GERRY: Your life's pretty good. Photo in the paper. Congratulations, you genius.

SUSANNAH: Genius…

GERRY: [*the gift*] I brought you this to mark the occasion.

SUSANNAH: You didn't have to…

GERRY: Hang on.

He shoots as she opens the gift, a CD.

SUSANNAH: I love her! How did you know? And it's my first CD.

GERRY: How do you feel? Twelve years of study and hard work and dreaming, and now these brilliant results. You can choose to do pretty much what you want to do. What will it be?

SUSANNAH: I'll do medicine. Probably I'll specialise, but in what I don't know, not yet. That's what I'm going to do. And naturally my parents are pleased. They always saw me in medicine. And that's where I'll be.

GERRY: Is that where you want to be?

SUSANNAH: The world needs good doctors.

GERRY: Is there something you'd rather be doing? What's in the book?

She stares at him, then picks up her journal.

SUSANNAH: My poetry.

GERRY: Do you want me to keep shooting? Last time we got to poetry, you made me stop.

SUSANNAH: Probably I was afraid it was terrible. Probably it's still terrible, but I now don't care. There's no one to mark it or assess it. I do it for myself. But I'd like to reach out with it. To reach someone else, you know?

She opens the book and starts to read, straight to camera.

'She's the one that watches,
Watches all the days and nights,

Watching, waiting to be seen and known,
Known for what she is, not what she seems to be,
Waiting to be seen and known,
Naked, pale as moonlight,
Trembling like leaves in a summer storm,
For the one who truly knows her,
The one who sees her soul,
To read what's long been written there—'

GERRY: Shit. Battery's gone. Sorry.

SUSANNAH: I can start again.

GERRY: I haven't got a spare with me. Sorry, Susannah.

SUSANNAH: Did you like it?

GERRY: It was beautiful. Beautiful. Now I'll give you beautiful. I'll tell
you about the people I found in Borneo.

◆ ◆ ◆ ◆ ◆

SCENE FIFTEEN: 1984

Zoe's house. ZOE *and* JESSIE *see Gerry's photographs of Borneo.*

JESSIE: It's one of the last rainforests. The Penan people are hunter-
gatherers. The forest is their home, it gives them their food, but the
Malaysian government is charging in there with bulldozers and
chainsaws—

ZOE: Jess, this is not my scene.

JESSIE: Animals will die. Man, a whole culture will die, so the Japanese
can turn these trees into wood-pulp.

ZOE: I couldn't afford it in a fit.

JESSIE: Gerry will lend you the dough. It won't cost that much. We'd be
living pretty rough.

ZOE: With Gerry?

JESSIE: Of course with Gerry. And the rest of the team.

ZOE: What would I say to Alex?

JESSIE: You're going bush with a bunch of mad greenies.

ZOE: And with Gerry.

JESSIE: It was his idea.

ZOE: So you're doing it for Gerry?

JESSIE: We're doing it for the Penan people. For all people.

ZOE: And for Gerry. He'll be taking his camera.

JESSIE: He wants to follow up on his last doco. It had an amazing response. SBS have put up some money—

ZOE: That stuff… it's you. It's not me.

> DOUG *emerges with a spanner.*

DOUG: It's done.

ZOE: Besides, I've got a job.

DOUG: You've got hot water.

ZOE: Thanks. This is Jessie—

JESSIE: Hi, Alex.

ZOE: Alex! This is Doug. Just a friend.

DOUG: Just a friend. I know all about you.

JESSIE: I'm trying to drag her off to Borneo.

ZOE: What do you think, Doug? [*To* JESSIE] He's like a total genius, so every time there's a crisis—

DOUG: She asks my advice, then follows her heart. Can I make us some tea?

ZOE: Great.

> DOUG *goes.*

Alex! You thought he was Alex? Does he even look like he's in a band!

JESSIE: He seems really nice.

ZOE: For a nerd. He's a law student. He sorted out all the insurance shit when we got ripped off.

JESSIE: And he gets your hot water running. What does Alex do?

ZOE: Alex makes music.

JESSIE: What does he do for you?

ZOE: He makes me feel needed.

JESSIE: Zozza, I need you on this one. I need a friend.

ZOE: You'll have Gerry. You follow your heart—

JESSIE: My heart isn't Gerry.

ZOE: You follow your heart, I follow mine. And mine doesn't say Borneo.

JESSIE: Does it ever say Jessie?

ZOE: That's not fair.

JESSIE: I never see you.

ZOE: It's never just you. There's always a banner. And nearly always a camera.

JESSIE: I miss you, bub.

ZOE: I have a life too.

JESSIE: I know.

ZOE: Have you ever come to hear Alex and the band? Alex is my life. Alex and his music.

JESSIE: I'll come. When we get back. Look… if you change your mind—

> DOUG *returns with tea and cups.*

DOUG: You know the bit I really like on your show? When you two get sprung having a pash.

JESSIE: He promised to stop using that.

ZOE: Are you kidding? It's in the promo. Every time.

JESSIE: Shame! [*To* DOUG] It wasn't a pash.

DOUG: Oh, right. How do you like your tea?

JESSIE: I've got to go. Bye, Zoe. [*To* DOUG] Good to meet you.

> *She kisses* ZOE *and goes. He looks at the Borneo stills.*

ZOE: Another bit of the world she's going to save.

DOUG: Was she a good kisser?

ZOE: Doug, get your hand off it.

◆ ◆ ◆ ◆ ◆

SCENE SIXTEEN: WINTER 1984

A cheering football crowd. Stadium. ANNIE *watches a game with* GERRY. *She is decked in team colours.* GERRY *films.*

GERRY: Yes, Cam. Go, Cam! Go, mate!

ANNIE: Has he told you much about me?

GERRY: Cam never says much about anything. He did say you're going sky-diving. I'll be there for that.

ANNIE: I bet you will.

He watches the game as ROGER *approaches.*

ROGER: Gerry!

GERRY: This is Annie. Annie, Roger.

ANNIE: I know you! Get the Maserati yet?

ROGER: That was a joke. How was Borneo?

GERRY: Mind-blowing. Scary. We did good things.

ROGER: [*to* ANNIE] Did you go to Borneo?

ANNIE: Borneo? I've never been further than Seal Rocks.

GERRY: Annie and I just met today.

ANNIE: Blind date, sort of thing.

She laughs. GERRY *laughs.*

ROGER: Oh. Nice. Who set you up?

ANNIE: Cam.

ROGER: You look good together.

ANNIE: Not too good, I hope. Me and Cam are going out together.

GERRY: Look at him! Go, Cam, go, mate! Great mark! Hey, Roger. Stand here, beside Annie.

He shoots the game past ROGER *and* ANNIE.

Beautiful. Keep your eyes on him…

He pans to focus on them. ROGER *stares at* GERRY.

Mate, eyes on the game.

ROGER: I didn't come for this…

ANNIE *starts screaming.*

ANNIE: Cam, you bloody beauty! Go, Swannies!

GERRY *swings round to shoot the field.* ANNIE *clutches* GERRY, *yelling. Pandemonium. On screen perhaps an image of* CAM *in muddy triumph on the field.*

◆ ◆ ◆ ◆ ◆

SCENE SEVENTEEN: DECEMBER 1985

December 1985. GERRY *is alone in Susannah's flat.*

GERRY: Nice place.

    SUSANNAH *emerges with drinks.*

SUSANNAH: My mother says it's a slum, so naturally I love it. My house-mates have gone to Byron. We've got the place to ourselves.

GERRY: Is this the annual celebration?

SUSANNAH: Of what?

GERRY: Another stack of brilliant results.

SUSANNAH: Gerry, I asked you to dinner. No celebration, just dinner. I do want to say something before we get too pissed. Thank you. That's it, that's what I had to say. Thank you.

GERRY: For what?

SUSANNAH: For a lot of things. One in particular. The day I read you my poem…

GERRY: Your poem? Oh, yes.

SUSANNAH: It was frightful, wasn't it?

GERRY: It was what it was.

SUSANNAH: It was tragic. So was I. But I was…

GERRY: Young.

SUSANNAH: Young, yes. But also—

GERRY: Vulnerable.

SUSANNAH: You keep finishing my sentences. Are you embarrassed?

GERRY: Possibly.

SUSANNAH: Possibly. Possibly you're embarrassed because possibly you remember that a big klutz of an eighteen-year-old girl—

GERRY: [*over* SUSANNAH] You were never a klutz.

SUSANNAH: —was possibly in love with you.

    Beat.

GERRY: In love?

SUSANNAH: Definitely. But I'm over it. The poetry thing. And the Gerry thing.

GERRY: Oh.

SUSANNAH: Am I hearing relief or disappointment?

GERRY: Isn't it always six of one…?

SUSANNAH: I'm relieved. I'm over you, Gerry.

GERRY: Okay.

SUSANNAH: Well and truly.

GERRY: Okay!

SUSANNAH: So now you can fuck me.

> *Silence.*

With impunity. Impunity… I was always the one with the superior vocab. I want to fuck you. Do you want to fuck me?

GERRY: Susannah, you're twenty, I'm forty-two. Twice your age. I'm old enough to be your father.

SUSANNAH: This is not transference, I don't want to sleep with my father, I want to fuck you. If you don't fancy me, we'll eat. But if you do… You do, don't you?

> *He nods. She laughs.*

My God, you do. I was trying it on. But you really do.

GERRY: Susannah, have you ever had a boyfriend?

SUSANNAH: You know I haven't, Gerry. You know everything about me. Every milestone has been yours for the taking, whatever that means.

GERRY: You haven't had a boyfriend.

SUSANNAH: I've been married to my studies. Now do a girl a favour. Help a poor virgin over the hump.

GERRY: But you're my… subject.

SUSANNAH: True. I'm your subject. But you're not my object. My object is experience. Give it to me.

GERRY: I don't know.

> *She puts a hand on his groin.*

SUSANNAH: This knows.

GERRY: What about the project?

SUSANNAH: The project. Only one more year to go. And I can keep a secret. Can you?

GERRY: I don't know…

SUSANNAH: Let's not worry about that. Not tonight.

She kisses him again. He kisses her.

◆ ◆ ◆ ◆ ◆

SCENE EIGHTEEN: DECEMBER 1985

ZOE *holds a baby.*

ZOE 20: [*on screen*] Yes, I was pregnant when we decided to get married. I wouldn't say a difficult decision, but it was a decision we thought about, to be parents. And I'm glad. Yes, surprised. Your life is heading in one direction, and something happens and you're picked up and dropped in another country. And you go, yes, I like it here. I'll stay.

Her partner joins her: DOUG 23.

DOUG 23: [*on screen*] It's the kind of happiness you dream about and suddenly it's yours. No, I didn't finish. That was an independent decision. I wasn't comfortable with the idea of practising law. I'm in the public service. But this is my life. Zoe and Sky.

◆ ◆ ◆ ◆ ◆

SCENE NINETEEN: 1985

Outside a restaurant, GERRY *has his camera.* CAM 20 *waves at the window.*

GERRY: She hasn't seen you yet.

CAM: Annie, look out here. See? Power of positive thinking.

GERRY: But will she come out?

CAM: She knows if she doesn't, I'll go in and give her heaps. Here she comes. Ready?

GERRY: I can't roll without asking her.

ANNIE *comes out in waitress uniform.*

ANNIE: You'll get me fired, you dork.

CAM: Roll, Gerry. Annie, something to tell you. I got the call. I got the offer.

ANNIE: Essendon. Right?

CAM: Yeah. How did you know!

ANNIE: It had to be Essendon, if it wasn't Collingwood. Well, good on you. [*To* GERRY] Am I meant to leap up and down? We know he's a champion. Now they'll know it down there.

CAM: If I'm playing for Essendon, I'll be moving to Melbourne.

ANNIE: It'd be hard to do it from here, wouldn't it?

CAM: Hate to leave you behind on your own.

ANNIE: I'll survive.

CAM: There's another option.

ANNIE: You turn down Collingwood.

CAM: In your dreams. I could take you with me.

ANNIE: Just like that?

CAM: No, I'll do the hard yards first. Annie…

He kneels and produces a small velvet-covered box.

You've been selected to join the Cam O'Brien team. Will you accept this transfer fee?

ANNIE: Get up, Cam.

CAM: We'll cover all your relocation costs, and find you suitable accommodation.

ANNIE: Stop it! Get up.

CAM: Say yes.

ANNIE: I've got things to say first. I won't be a footie widow.

CAM: No way.

ANNIE: And I won't bring up kids on my own. That's a job for two—

CAM: I should have brought a bloody lawyer.

ANNIE: If your life goes the way I think it'll go—

He kisses her. She resists.

Listen to me. Gerry, make him listen.

GERRY *moves closer.*

What's happening here?

CAM: What's happening? You've just been proposed to on national TV. Kiss me.

> *She kisses him.*

ANNIE: Piss off, Gerry.

> *But* GERRY *moves in closer.*

❖ ❖ ❖ ❖ ❖

SCENE TWENTY: EDITING ROOM, DECEMBER 1985

JESSIE 20: [*on screen*] I'm in relationships with a lot of people. You mean, am I sleeping with anyone? I like what I'm doing. I like my course. A Diploma in Community Health. I wouldn't call myself that, I wouldn't call myself an activist. You might. Young koori activist, who said that? I'm not even a koori. My mother's a Torres Strait Islander. My dad reckons he comes from good old convict stock, so what does that make me? Jessie. Just Jessie. Music, dancing, eating, a bit of study, letting life happen. I like my life, you know? Yes, that's it, that's where I am. I like my life. Do you like your life?

> GERRY *watches the edited footage. He replays the tape, cutting the last phrase so the grab ends thus:*

Yes, that's it, that's where I am. I like my life.

❖ ❖ ❖ ❖ ❖

SCENE TWENTY-ONE: STREET, 26 JANUARY 1986

THEO *follows* JESSIE.

THEO: Jessie? Hey, Jessie.

JESSIE: Yes?

THEO: Good meeting, eh? Really positive.

JESSIE: Yes.

THEO: And you run things really well.

JESSIE: Thanks… uh… sorry…

THEO: Theo. You're very inclusive. I thought you'd be more controlling. I've seen you speaking a rallies and stuff, and you come across as—

JESSIE: Theo—

THEO: Very together, very strong—

JESSIE: Is this going somewhere?

THEO: Yes, I'm trying to find a cool way to crack on to you. That's a joke.

JESSIE: Good one. Well, see you next time…

THEO: Hey. I'm hungry. Are you hungry?

JESSIE: Yes, but I'm also broke. True. No money.

THEO: No worries. I'm a chef. I cook at my uncle's joint. I'll make you good Greek food.

JESSIE: I'm a vegetarian.

THEO: Good Greek vegetarian food.

JESSIE: Sounds great. But if you are cracking on—

THEO: Hey, I want to be your friend.

JESSIE: Good. So long as you don't mean boyfriend—

THEO: It's out there! The B word!

JESSIE: Because I'm not up for a boyfriend.

THEO: Are you gay?

JESSIE: Or a girlfriend. But I am on for a feed.

THEO: I'll feed you. Beautiful. This is destiny.

JESSIE: No, just dinner.

THEO: You've been like my mantra.

JESSIE: Get out of it.

THEO: 'I want time to be all the things that I can be. None of us want that time taken from us. We want our chance at life.' New Year's Day 1981. You were talking to me.

JESSIE: Jesus—

THEO: I knew some day I had to meet you.

JESSIE: He's a stalker.

THEO: He's someone on the great journey of life. And he found a kindred spirit. I feel I know you like a friend.

JESSIE: But you don't.

THEO: And now I can return the favour. You can get to know me.

JESSIE: That's big of you.

THEO: I'm a big man. You'll see. Come on, a Greek dinner on Australia Day. Perfect.

JESSIE: Not for a blackfella. We don't even like the name.

THEO: Then forget Australia Day. It's our day. Our night. I'll do you beans and okra and eggplant—

GERRY *approaches in a dinner jacket.*

JESSIE: Gerry! And all duded up. How come?

GERRY: Somehow I knew you'd forget.

JESSIE: Forget what? Gerry Hilferty, this is Theo— [*To* THEO] What's your last name?

THEO: Theodosopoulos.

JESSIE: So what's your first name?

THEO: Apollo.

JESSIE: Apollo? Apollo!

THEO: Theo will do just fine. Gerard Hilferty…

THEO *and* GERRY *shake hands.*

The man with five children.

GERRY: That's me. [*To* JESSIE] It's Roger's twenty-first.

THEO: Roger? The one with everything that opens and—

GERRY: That's him. Our first twenty-first. Come on, Jess.

JESSIE: I've just been offered a free feed.

GERRY: There might be a few scraps of food at the Regent.

JESSIE: I'm not dressed up.

GERRY: We'll spin by your place.

THEO: Why don't I feed you both first?

GERRY: We're late already.

JESSIE: Couldn't you go without me?

GERRY: You accepted, Jess.

JESSIE: [*to* THEO] I'm sorry. Another time.

THEO: You better believe it.

THEO *waves and goes.*

GERRY: Nice guy. New friend?

JESSIE: Yes.

GERRY: Your new friend Apollo. Let's get you scrubbed up for your old friend Roger.

◆ ◆ ◆ ◆ ◆

SCENE TWENTY-TWO: NEW YEAR'S DAY 1987

In Zoe's house: DOUG 24, ZOE, SUSANNAH, JESSIE, ROGER, CAM *and* ANNIE 21, *and* GERRY 43 *watch* ROGER *on TV.*

ROGER 21: [*on screen*] Dad says that by the time you add up all the school bills and the dentist's bills and the maths coaching, I must be the most expensive construction project he's ever worked on. But he was paying for this one. Well, the job's done, and I'm open for business. I'd like to thank my good friend Jessie for the beautiful speech. You'll recognise Jessie from her supporting role in my movies. Seriously, we've been through fourteen years together, two-thirds of our lives, and Gerry's been there for every major moment, even when you wish he wasn't.

> *On a screen, a new sportscar stands in a driveway.* ROGER *is blindfolded, then the car is revealed to him. At the party, all laugh at this,* ROGER *the loudest. Then...*

SUSANNAH 21: [*on screen*] No, I won't miss it. But it's odd to leave it at this point. Twenty-one is not the end of anything. If we kept going, it could get really challenging. Sooner or later, one of us would rock the boat. So this is Susannah signing off. I've got two more years to go, a year of residency, then I'll specialise. I'm thinking about psychiatry. I blame you. Just kidding. That's a funny phrase to end on. 'I blame you.'

> *All laugh at this,* SUSANNAH *loudest. On screen, images of* ZOE *with* DOUG *and their baby;* CAM *and* ANNIE 21 *on their wedding day, clowning for the camera; then* JESSIE *is heard at 14 at the rally.*

JESSIE 14: I want time to be all the things that I can be. None of us want that time taken from us. We want our chance at life.

The telecast is over.

SUSANNAH: And that, boys and girls, is the end of the story.

DOUG: Wow. I feel I've known Zoe all her life.

GERRY: What do you feel, Zoe?

ZOE: Glad I've finished something.

ANNIE: So that's it? Over and out?

SUSANNAH: That was the deal. One day a year till we got to twenty-one.

ANNIE: But you said it's odd to be finishing.

SUSANNAH: Did I? When?

ANNIE: Up there. On the screen.

JESSIE: Gerry, you must want to start something new.

GERRY: Yes, I do.

JESSIE: Good. Let's drink to something new. For Gerry, for all of us…

They all raise their glasses… except GERRY.

GERRY: But Susannah's right. It's odd to finish now. Doug says he feels he's known Zoe all her life, and I'm thinking, all her life? It's scarcely begun.

ZOE: Thanks.

GERRY: Like all our lives. It's work in progress. Zoe has a daughter. Most of you, maybe all of you will have kids. What a gift for them, to see their parents as people, continuing to evolve.

ZOE: That could be a reason for us to go on. What about you?

GERRY: I look around this group tonight and I'm thinking, who did I sell short? What did I miss? Where did I skimp? Still, we've brought you to twenty-one. And tonight a couple of million people saw Roger and his Maserati, Jessie at her land rights rally, Cam and Annie's celebrity wedding, Doug and Zoe's baby, Susannah choosing psychiatry and blaming me. Now we could go deeper. We could show that every one of you is on the same journey, the one we're all on. But that will take time.

ZOE: How much time?

GERRY: I'd like to be with you for another decade.

SUSANNAH: Another decade?

GERRY: A few more careers launched, a few more babies born, five adult lives in process. Another ten years or so, and I'd be ready to move on to something new. And we could drink that toast then.

JESSIE: Ten years or so…

GERRY: You might want to discuss this. I'll leave the room.

ROGER: Do you have to know tonight?

GERRY: You're all here together. Seize the moment. Talk to each other. Decide.

> GERRY *goes out of the room. Silence.*

CAM: Well? Anyone got a problem?

ROGER: I'm sick of being a national joke.

ZOE: You're not, Roger.

ROGER: You were all laughing tonight.

CAM: You were laughing harder than anyone. We've all made idiots of ourselves. Annie let me propose to her on TV!

ANNIE: I didn't have much choice.

CAM: You loved it. She loved it. Mate, it's all a big game.

ROGER: So Cam's in for another ten years. Does anyone else want to go on?

JESSIE: Not me. Not really.

ROGER: See?

JESSIE: But if Gerry wants to keep going, I can't say no. It means too much to him.

ROGER: So you're doing it for him?

ZOE: We'll do it for Sky. If Doug's happy.

DOUG: Whatever you think, Zoe. I think Sky'll enjoy it.

CAM: 'Course she will. I want my kids to see it all, see me the day my mum died, see me scrapping with you [*Roger*] —

ANNIE: [*to* CAM] You coming out of the cop shop.

CAM: —see me coming out of the cop shop, see me pashing their mum. That's the game. Come on, mate. One in, all in.

ROGER: Of course you'll be in it. You're a celebrity.

CAM: So I don't need this. I've got cameras coming at me day and night. But I'll do it for him.

ROGER: I won't.

CAM: Too gutless?

ROGER: Gutless. Funny word, if it's all just a big game.

CAM: Don't tell me you haven't enjoyed the ride. Mate, you're the celebrity.

>ROGER *scoffs.*

Fair dinkum. You're the one the journos ask about.

ROGER: Because I'm the one they label.

CAM: Turn them around. You'll feel heaps better. I did. Mate, when you look back and see where I was headed—

ROGER: Jessie? What are you thinking? What should I do?

JESSIE: Have you got stuff to say to Gerry?

>*Beat. Then* ROGER *nods.*

You might want the chance to say it.

ROGER: Yes, I might.

ZOE: Tell the full story. That's what I want to do.

ROGER: Yes.

CAM: On ya, mate. He's in.

ROGER: Yes, mate. Looks like he is.

CAM: [*to* SUSANNAH] What about you, Susannah?

SUSANNAH: I won't be the one who bailed. I won't give him that satisfaction. He'd follow the four of you, and I'd be a shadow.

ZOE: What does that mean?

SUSANNAH: I'll give him his ten years. Or so.

CAM: [*calling*] Gerry, they're in!

>CAM *and* ANNIE *have gone.*

JESSIE: Ten years or so. Well, there we are.

SUSANNAH: There we are. Five blind mice. See how they run.

❖ ❖ ❖ ❖ ❖

SCENE TWENTY-THREE: MELBOURNE, SUMMER 1988

On a screen an image of CAM 23 *accepting an award.* GERRY *emerges with* CAM *from the post-award party.*

CAM: Mate. Did you clock the blonde at the bar? Total fox.

GERRY: Red dress?

CAM: Name's Shannon. I gave her your number.

GERRY: My number? In Sydney?

CAM: No, here, dickhead. St Kilda.

GERRY: She wants to fuck me?

CAM: No, mate! Me. And I can't call her. There's a boyfriend. She'll ring you in one hour. Give her your address—

GERRY: Cam, do you want to borrow my place to—?

CAM: Don't give me shit. It's not like an affair.

GERRY: No, but—

CAM: You saw her. How do I say no to that?

GERRY: Couldn't you go to a hotel?

CAM: And tomorrow it's all over town. This way no one gets hurt.

> *They see* ANNIE *approaching. She's pregnant.*

Throw me a line. Any line.

GERRY: Jesus, Cam—

CAM: You took your time.

ANNIE: You don't have to queue to take a pee.

CAM: That's one great thing about being born with a dick.

ANNIE: One of the many.

GERRY: Thanks for a great night. Congratulations, again. Bye, Annie.

CAM: See you round.

GERRY: Yeah.

> *Beat.* CAM *stares.*

CAM: Been a good night, eh? [*Beat.*] Get some good stuff? I'll always give you good stuff. [*Beat.*] Always did. Always will.

GERRY: Cammo, that reminds me. Those old tapes. I need them back.

ANNIE: What tapes?

CAM: All our kid stuff. The out-takes.

ANNIE: I've never seen them.

CAM: One day. [*To* GERRY] When do you need them, mate?

GERRY: Tonight. If possible.

CAM: Tonight? Shit. I'll drop Annie home and bring them over.

ANNIE: You've got the magic touch, Gerry. I can't get him to go to Prahran Market.

◆ ◆ ◆ ◆ ◆

SCENE TWENTY-FOUR: 1988

ROGER 23: [*on screen*] Apparently I wanted to be a pilot, an engineer, a designer of pinball machines, whatever. I can't remember saying any of that. My dad's opened an office in Hong Kong. I might go

Travis McMahon as Cam and Justine Clarke as Annie in the 2002 Sydney Theatre Company production. (Photo: Heidrun Löhr)

and work there. I'd have to learn Cantonese. I think I'd like hotel management. People tell me I'd be good in the hospitality industry. I play the markets a bit, make money some days. I go clubbing. But the women I like don't go for Asian men, so I end up with… I want to travel, but I wouldn't want to go overseas on my own. What I really like to do is… I get in my car and I drive. And I keep driving.

◆ ◆ ◆ ◆ ◆

SCENE TWENTY-FIVE: 26 JANUARY 1988

Jessie's house. On the floor THEO *and* GERRY *staple a banner to two poles.*

THEO: I'm stoked. This will be an epic day, eh?

GERRY: What happens afterwards?

THEO: Total enlightenment, a national apology, proper land rights legislation—

GERRY: That'd be great, Theo, but I meant tonight.

THEO: There'll be a party somewhere. Stick with us.

GERRY: I'd like some time with you.

THEO: With a whitefella? You need the koori perspective.

GERRY: I'll get that. But I'm shooting for myself as well. It's all right, Jess agreed. It's a trade-off. I shoot the march and the meeting for the group. And I get some stuff with Jess. And you, I hope.

THEO: Me? Why me?

GERRY: Well, now you're living together—

THEO: Me and Jessie? We don't live together.

GERRY: Looks like you are. Every time I'm here—

THEO: You see me cooking. If I don't cook, she doesn't eat. I've got my own place, I don't live here. Well, I live here, pretty much, I just don't sleep here. Oh! Jess and me? Gotcha. No, we're just mates.

GERRY: Still, you're in her life. I'd like you in the project.

JESSIE *comes in.*

JESSIE: Come on, boys, time to hit the road.

GERRY: Aren't you going to brief me first?

JESSIE: No need. Get down there with the crowd. Talk to the aunties and uncles, talk to the young ones, ask what they're thinking. Go with your gut.

THEO: Ready. Roll from my end…

They hoist the banner. Painted with traditional symbols, it reads: 'Two Hundred Years of Survival'.

JESSIE: Beautiful. Come on.

THEO *and* GERRY *roll the banner.*

GERRY: I'd like some time at the end of the day. With both of you.

THEO: No. Not me.

GERRY: Why not?

JESSIE: Whitepella come steal his spirit. Let's move it. The traffic will be hell.

JESSIE *goes out.* THEO *is following.*

GERRY: Theo, I'd be really grateful—

THEO: Mate. It's not my gig. I'm not in your story.

GERRY: Would you talk about her? On camera?

THEO: Jess is right. That thing can steal your spirit.

GERRY: Say that, then. Challenge the whole project.

THEO: Mate, you're good. Come on.

GERRY: If you're in Jessie's life—

THEO: Heaps of people in Jessie's life. This house is one big sitdown. Anyway, you've got five kids to keep you happy.

GERRY: Always room for one more.

THEO: Too late, Gerry. I came along too late.

◆ ◆ ◆ ◆ ◆

SCENE TWENTY-SIX: 1989

ZOE 24: [*on screen*] When I do this now, I'm doing it for my daughter. She'll watch this, even when I'm dead, and she'll know what I was thinking. That's if I know what I'm thinking. 'Not going anywhere'? Is that what I said? I don't remember. I mean I don't remember her, that girl. I think I'm going somewhere. I don't know where, but somewhere. We'll see. She'll see. My daughter will see.

◆ ◆ ◆ ◆ ◆

SCENE TWENTY-SEVEN: 1989

Beach. Coast of NSW. ROGER 24 *catches* GERRY. *Both have been jogging.* ROGER *is out of breath.*

ROGER: I'm having an ozone rush. Talk about a natural high.

GERRY: Nothing like it.

ROGER: It's awesome. This view. You and me. No camera. And we're in your space.

GERRY: This space belongs to the nation. To the Wiradjuri Nation, if we're really honest.

ROGER: But it's your world, the place where you get it sorted out. The city's killing me. This is all I need, sea and sky and space.

GERRY: It's easy enough to find.

ROGER: I can't do it on my own. I tried that in Hong Kong. I lasted six months. Now I've blown it with Dad. He flew me home and laid on the big guilt trip, I've-given-you-everything-and-I'm-seeing-nothing. Then he introduced me to his stockbroker and handed me four hundred grand. What I didn't stick up my nose went down the toilet. I lost everything but the car. You need a car if you're dealing in Sydney.

GERRY: Mate…

ROGER: I told you, it's killing me. Gerry, could I… could I come and stay here?

GERRY: Here? Sure. I'm away working next month. You can house-sit.

ROGER: I wouldn't trust myself alone here. When you get back, could I come then?

GERRY: Come and stay with me?

ROGER: Just for a while. [*He finds his cigarettes and lights up.*] So I can see how you do it.

Kenneth Moraleda as Roger in the 2002 Sydney Theatre Company production. (Photo: Heidrun Löhr)

GERRY: Do what?

ROGER: How you work. How you live.

GERRY: Rog… You need to live your own life, not mine.

ROGER: I need to live my own life.

GERRY: Yes.

ROGER: Do it on my own.

GERRY: Yes.

ROGER: Is that what you told Cam? When you turned his life around?

GERRY: I never turned it around.

ROGER: You let him stay for three months, you found him a job—

GERRY: How do you know that?

ROGER: We all knew. You took him in, why not me?

GERRY: He was sixteen. You're twenty-four. I can't direct your life.

ROGER: For the last ten years I couldn't go anywhere without somebody staring and pointing. That's him, that's Roger, the Maserati kid. And then on my twenty-first you set me up. And you don't direct my life. I asked you not to show the presents.

GERRY: I had to show the car. It was part of your story.

ROGER: It was the whole story for you.

GERRY: No, Rog. But I'm sorry it upset you.

ROGER: No, you're not. You show what you want to show. You know how the Chinese make pots? There's always one mistake, one crack to show how perfect the rest of it is. That's me.

GERRY: Mate, don't be such a fucking wuss! Whose life is perfect?

ROGER: Cam's must be pretty close.

GERRY: I helped Cam because he had nobody. Nobody and nothing. You've had a mother and father and a nanny and two sisters—

ROGER: And I'm still lonely.

GERRY: Who isn't, mate? Smarten up. Get yourself a project.

ROGER: I'll find one. Help me. You're my Obi Wan Kenobe. You showed me talking to that toy, but you're the real thing. Let me come and stay.

GERRY: Roger, nobody stays down here. It's my private space.

ROGER: Is this where you fucked Susannah? You did fuck her, didn't you?

GERRY: Did she tell you that?

ROGER: No, but you just did.

GERRY: I've said nothing.

ROGER: I knew already. I saw how she was with you. I took photos, and when they came out, I saw heaps of things. Then I looked back at the films, I've got the whole thing on tape, and I saw even more. I worked out my role.

GERRY: Your role? I don't make drama, nobody has roles.

ROGER: Everybody has roles. There's one you've adopted, one you love—

GERRY: You think I was in love with Susannah?

ROGER: One you love, and one you hate.

GERRY: You think that's your role? I don't hate you, Roger.

ROGER: But if something bad had to happen to one of us—

GERRY: Don't do this to yourself—

ROGER: It should probably be—

GERRY: Roger. Stop it. Get out of here.

ROGER: See? You do hate me.

GERRY: I don't. Listen to me. Get out. Go somewhere and grow up.

ROGER: Overseas? I've been—

GERRY: Overseas, the outback, wherever. Somewhere with no clubs, no drugs, no parties, no cars. No shit. Somewhere with nothing. Go and test yourself. Do it tough. I'll lend you some dough.

ROGER: You're pushing me out of your life.

GERRY: No. I'll make you a promise. You go, and when you're ready, when you send me a sign, I'll come. We'll spend time. Wherever you are, I'll come.

ROGER: Without a camera?

GERRY: I wouldn't be me without a camera.

◆ ◆ ◆ ◆ ◆

SCENE TWENTY-EIGHT: 1990

GERRY *finishes shooting* SUSANNAH 25 *in academic gown at her graduation.*

SUSANNAH: Another visit to the zoo. Today we feed the baby doctors.

GERRY: And when feeding time is over?

SUSANNAH: I take up a fellowship in the School of Paediatrics at Johns Hopkins in Baltimore.

GERRY: Not psychiatry?

SUSANNAH: Not psychiatry, that would have been too perfect. Paediatrics. My new life. So this is Susannah signing off.

She sings.

'Ma chandelle est morte, je n'ai plus de feu.'

Put the camera down, Gerry. My turn to ask you something.

He puts the camera down.

What happened between us... did that mean anything to you?

GERRY: It was... nice. But I felt I'd crossed some line. I felt... ashamed.

SUSANNAH: Is that why you've never said anything?

GERRY: Was there anything to be said?

SUSANNAH: You were out of there before dawn, and then it was as though it never happened. Not one word in four years.

GERRY: But you told me it meant nothing.

Steve Bisley as Gerry and Genevieve O'Reilly as Susannah in the 2002 Sydney Theatre Company production. (Photo: Heidrun Löhr)

SUSANNAH: To make it easier for you.

GERRY: That wasn't true?

SUSANNAH: That wasn't true, and by the end of the night you must have known it. You saw how needy I was…

GERRY: Susannah? Were you really… you know, in love?

SUSANNAH: You know, I really was. And I hoped you'd see that. But you didn't see. Not when it mattered. You see when you want to see, when you're shooting. You saw that silly poem I wrote. You see us all so clearly until you put that thing down. And then you can't see what you've put on the screen for millions of strangers to see. You can't read your own work.

GERRY: I have to. I edit it, inch by inch.

SUSANNAH: But do you read what's there? It's like a journal. And you know something? One page in five is a valentine.

GERRY: A valentine?

SUSANNAH: Once a year, a love letter on the screen. Goodbye, Gerry.

He stares at her. On screen, perhaps an image of JESSIE?

❖ ❖ ❖ ❖ ❖

SCENE TWENTY-NINE: JESSIE'S HOUSE, 1990

GERRY: Your street's so… what's that bloody word? Gentrified.

JESSIE: Not this house. We're the last hold-out.

GERRY: You look great. Glowing.

JESSIE: You don't look that flash.

GERRY: I've been hard at it, Jess.

JESSIE: Are you here for the project? I wish you'd warned me.

GERRY: No. No project. I wanted to see how you are.

JESSIE: You got it. Glowing. You know why?

GERRY: You're not greedy. You're not needy. You're happy.

JESSIE: Yes, I'm happy. Gerry, I've got news.

GERRY: Me too. I don't know where to start.

JESSIE: Then I'll go first.

GERRY: No! Me. Please? Big stuff. I want to get it out.

JESSIE: Go for your life.

GERRY: Jessie… It's hard for me to see you here and now. You're so many pictures in my head. When I started out, it was a level playing field, you know? Five children. You could go any way, do anything, and I'd follow. The network gave me money, I kept delivering, every year, New Year's Day, and there'd be more money and on we'd go, and I saw some things I shouldn't have seen, I missed some things I should have seen, and of course I did other jobs, and I went to interesting places, Borneo, remember? You and me sleeping side by side on that concrete floor, that was a good gig, there were lots of them, and I did them well, but they were only what I did while I was waiting… waiting to do what I was meant to do. My own journal. My *Five Children*. I kept at it. And the shows went deeper every time, I know you never see them, but they're good, they reach people, I get amazing letters, and… I'm lost… Where did I start? A level playing field. Five children, five stories. But one story kept growing… keeps growing. [*Beat.*] Jessie…

JESSIE: What?

GERRY: Your story. On screen it's Jessie and then the others. Susannah made me see. It's you. I'm interested in the others, I care about them, I like them. But you… I love you. Probably I always have. I mean, since… What does it matter? What matters is I can't get you out of my head. The way you look, the way you think, the fire inside you. I don't know whether you even like men, let alone this man, and I'm twenty years older than you—

JESSIE: Gerry, listen—

GERRY: I'd give up the project. I'd put it to rest. I've got a life, I can do other things. So long as I'm with you. I'm yours, Jess. If you—

Voices and laughter outside.

You're expecting people?

JESSIE: Gerry, I've been trying to tell you…

GERRY: There's someone else.

JESSIE: There's a baby. I'm having a baby. True.

ZOE *arrives with flowers.*

GERRY: Zoe. Hi. You're having a baby? On your own?

THEO *brings bags of food.*

JESSIE: With Theo.

GERRY: Congratulations. But you were…

THEO: Mates, yeah.

JESSIE: We still are, but we… moved on.

Silence. GERRY *embraces* JESSIE, *then* THEO.

THEO: Hope you're hungry, mate. I'm cooking. Big celebration. Had our first ultrasound today, didn't we, Jess?

JESSIE: You will stay?

GERRY: I didn't mean to gatecrash. I dropped by to…

JESSIE: To discuss our next thrilling instalment.

ZOE: *Five Children Have Children…*

THEO: Just make mine look stunning.

ZOE: This one'll want to shoot the birth.

She takes the flowers out.

GERRY: I'll leave you to it.

THEO: No way, mate. You brought us together. How you could make someone look that cool at fourteen…

GERRY: I could have done it for you, Theo.

THEO: No one could do it for me at fourteen. I was tragic. Round shoulders, pebble glasses and five o'clock shadow. Then Jess discovered she couldn't live without me, and my inner beauty was unleashed on the world. See?

THEO *takes the food out.* JESSIE *looks steadily at* GERRY *then kisses him.*

JESSIE: Would you really have given up the project?

ZOE *brings the flowers in.*

Zoe, where's your mob?

ZOE: Doug's parking. But no Sky, she's having a sleepover with Amy, her bestest best friend in the universe. Pizza and videos and a Barbie doll with a new range of slumberwear. Your ultrasound photos couldn't compete. Look, Gerry's staring. Is it the hair?

GERRY: I've never heard you talk so long without drawing breath.

ZOE: Well, you live and learn.

> DOUG *arrives with champagne.*

DOUG: Hi, Jess.

ZOE: Doesn't she look fantastic?

DOUG: Glowing.

> *He embraces* JESSIE.

Where's the camera, Gerry?

GERRY: No camera tonight.

ZOE: No wonder Gerry looks lost. Don't you think? Jess? Like a little boy, lost without his big toy.

> *Silence.* GERRY *looks at his watch.*

GERRY: I have to go.

JESSIE: Please stay.

> THEO *brings food.*

GERRY: I have to be somewhere else.

> GERRY *hurries out.* JESSIE *goes to follow, changes her mind.*
>
> *On the screen, images of* THE FIVE CHILDREN *at 7, coming to rest at* JESSIE.

END OF ACT ONE

Genevieve O'Reilly as Susannah and Steve Bisley as Gerry in the 2002
Sydney Theatre Company production. (Photo: Heidrun Löhr)

ACT TWO

SCENE THIRTY: OUT OF TIME

ROGER *walks in* GERRY*'s dream.*

ROGER: Gerry? Gerry?

GERRY: Roger…

ROGER: Will you come for me? You said you'd come when I called.

GERRY: Where are you? Where did you go?

ROGER: Where you told me to go.

GERRY: Where? Where, Roger?

ROGER: Somewhere far away. Somewhere with nothing. Will you come for me?

GERRY: Where are you?

> ROGER *is gone.*

◆ ◆ ◆ ◆ ◆

SCENE THIRTY-ONE: OUTSIDE A CLUB, NIGHT, MELBOURNE, 1991

CAM 26 *pursues* ZOE.

ZOE: Let go of me.

CAM: I saw you checking me out—

ZOE: I know you—

CAM: Everyone fucken knows me—

ZOE: And you know me, Cam. Wake up to yourself!

> *She pushes him away as* GERRY *emerges from the club.*

GERRY: Come on, babe. Tonight you can shag a living legend.

ZOE: Gerry, look at me!

GERRY: Zoe.

CAM: Fuck me. What have you come as!

GERRY: I like it. Don't go. Stay for a drink.

ZOE: Then I can shag a living legend?

CAM: If you play your cards right.

ZOE: I'm not a player, Cam.

CAM: Bullshit. You were picking up in there.

ZOE: Was I?

CAM: So you can score an old mate. Or two.

GERRY: Cam, shut up. Zoe, why don't you stay for one more?

ZOE: No, why don't I go home, and you can do each other?

CAM: Eh? What did she say?

GERRY: Shut up. What are you doing in Melbourne?

ZOE: I came down for a funeral.

GERRY: I didn't know you had family here.

ZOE: It wasn't family. It was Alex.

GERRY: Alex. Boyfriend Alex? Lead guitar Alex?

> *She nods.*

I'm sorry. Accident?

ZOE: More or less. AIDS.

GERRY: Was that a shock?

ZOE: I'd been visiting him for months. We just had the wake. He used to play here. Goodnight.

CAM: Stay and we'll cheer you up, have a few drinks.

ZOE: You've had enough, mate. [*To* GERRY] Aren't you a bit old for joints like this?

GERRY: I'm keeping an eye on him.

ZOE: You're in no state to keep an eye on anyone.

GERRY: Hang on, Zoe. Talk to me. Tell me… how's Jessie?

ZOE: How do you think? Sad.

GERRY: Sad? What about?

ZOE: How long since you've talked to her? Their baby—

GERRY: They lost the baby.

ZOE: She miscarried a month ago.

GERRY: Oh, God.

ZOE: She's okay. But devastated, they both are. Call them. See them. And get Cam home before he does real damage.

ZOE *goes.*

GERRY: Jessie lost her child.

CAM: Real damage.

GERRY: She lost her child.

CAM: Shit happens.

GERRY: She lost her baby and I didn't know.

CAM: She'll have another one. They always do, look at my missus. What did that cunt mean, real damage?

GERRY: You do damage, Cammo. To other people. To yourself.

CAM: Don't talk to me like a fucken kid.

GERRY: You're a grown man. Sometimes you're a wild man.

CAM: And you love being there.

GERRY: Not tonight. I'm going home.

CAM: No way.

GERRY: If you love someone, they're in your life…

CAM: What?

GERRY: Nothing. See you, Cam…

CAM: Come on. I'll drive you.

GERRY: No, you won't.

CAM: Yes, I will. We have to talk. You said, you said I do damage. You're going to tell me how.

GERRY: Not tonight, mate.

CAM: If not tonight, never. I fucken mean it, man.

Silence. CAM *walks away. Then* GERRY *walks after him.*

GERRY: Hey, Cammo. Wait…

◆ ◆ ◆ ◆ ◆

SCENE THIRTY-TWO:
ZOE AND DOUG'S HOUSE, SYDNEY, NEXT NIGHT, 1991

The TV plays silently. Neither DOUG *nor* ZOE *watches it.*

DOUG: Zoe, I'm sorry about Alex. Very sorry. Nobody should die like that. But he's not part of Sky's life, alive or dead. He gave up that claim when he shot through on her.

ZOE: But I don't like to think we're withholding something—

DOUG: From a six-year-old? Of course we are.

ZOE: I don't mean we should tell her now!

DOUG: When? When she's seven? Eight? Nine?

ZOE: I don't know. But sometime.

DOUG: My name is on her birth certificate.

ZOE: We did agree—

DOUG: When there was a reason—

ZOE: We'd tell her one day—

DOUG: When there was a reason. Now there's no longer a reason. Be fair. I'm the one at risk.

ZOE: She'll know you wanted her. Where's the risk in that?

DOUG: I don't want to talk about it.

ZOE: Well, I do.

DOUG: Don't you understand? I have to believe she's my child. I gave up a lot for her.

ZOE: Yes, but she will need to know one day.

DOUG: I gave up my law course for her. And for you.

ZOE: You told Gerry—

DOUG: What else could I say? Someone had to be the breadwinner.

> ZOE*'s eye is caught by the TV screen.*

I deserve some credit for that, don't I? Zoe?

ZOE: Turn it up. Quick. That's Cam.

> DOUG *picks up the remote.*

I saw him last night with Gerry, after the wake… Oh, God. Oh, God. No.

They see, and perhaps we see, an image of a wrecked sports car.

NEWS REPORTER: [*voice-over*] O'Brien was at the wheel of this vehicle when it crashed into a parked car in Punt Road in the early hours of this morning. O'Brien was admitted to Royal Melbourne Hospital in a critical condition, and is undergoing emergency surgery. Also injured was his passenger, film-maker Gerard Hilferty whose TV series *Five Children* made Cam O'Brien a well-known Australian face even before he achieved his current status as AFL legend.

On the screen, images of CAM...

CAM 10: [*voice-over*] Carn, Wests! Carn, Wests!

CAM 18: [*voice-over*] I hear this roaring, and I know, that's for me.

CAM 20: [*voice-over*] Your first Grand Final? It's better than sex, mate.

ZOE: No more death. Please.

◆ ◆ ◆ ◆ ◆

SCENE THIRTY-THREE: 1992

GERRY *with* SUSANNAH. *He limps, using a stick.*

SUSANNAH: Poor Cam. Poor Annie.

GERRY: It'll be a struggle. The kids are taking it pretty well.

SUSANNAH: And Roger? What's happened to Roger?

GERRY: Last heard of in Marrakesh. A year ago. Then nothing. It's as if...

He's silent. Perhaps he sees Roger? SUSANNAH *doesn't. She studies* GERRY.

As if something happened. And I don't know what it is.

SUSANNAH: How maddening for you.

GERRY: I told him to go away. He went away. And he kept going. I've lost him.

SUSANNAH: Till he wants to be found.

GERRY: I miss him. I suppose that's why...

SUSANNAH: Why what?

He starts to shoot.

GERRY: I never expected to see you back here. Are you going to teach?

SUSANNAH: For a while I thought that might be my life, but then they asked us to volunteer in a neighbourhood clinic. I spent my summers doing that. Summer in the projects in Baltimore, go figure. I saw enough to know I wouldn't be happy in academia. I came back to work in public health. As soon as I've had my baby.

GERRY: Are you planning to get pregnant?

SUSANNAH: I am pregnant. Did you think I'd just stacked on the weight?

He puts down the camera.

GERRY: You're having a child?

SUSANNAH: And I couldn't be happier. You can shoot this, Gerry.

◆ ◆ ◆ ◆ ◆

SCENE THIRTY-FOUR: EDITING ROOM, 1992

GERRY *works alone.*

SUSANNAH 27: [*on screen*] I came back to work in public health. As soon as I've had my baby. No, I'm having it alone. I haven't found out the sex. I decided not to. I've got a name for either eventuality. Gabriel. I do the pre-natal classes, and they say: but you'd know so much, being a doctor, and a paediatrician. I know something. But what comes out, that's as big a mystery to me as to anyone. I'm excited. No, I don't think they'll be in conflict, my life and my work. You need both, and I'll have them. Maybe for the first time. Happiness is a dangerous word. I'll say I'm enjoying my life. Are you enjoying yours? I said, are you enjoying yours?

She looks directly at the camera. GERRY *rewinds and edits. Then the footage ends thus...*

Happiness is a dangerous word. I'll say I'm enjoying my life.

◆ ◆ ◆ ◆ ◆

SCENE THIRTY-FIVE:
BACKYARD, ANNIE AND CAM'S HOUSE, SYDNEY, 1993

GERRY *is alone for a moment.*

GERRY: It's nice. Good big yard for the kids. You've done well.

ANNIE *brings* CAM *out in a wheelchair.*

ANNIE: We couldn't have found anything without my dad. He's been a champion, hasn't he, Cam?

Silence.

GERRY: You've got a good colour, mate.

ANNIE: He's had a bit of sun. Haven't you? Dad put those ramps in. Cam gets in and out of the place like nobody's business.

CAM *wheels himself away.*

GERRY: If you need money—

ANNIE: We couldn't take it, Gerry. Not after what you went through.

GERRY: I'd like to help.

ANNIE: We're doing okay. We've got a roof over our heads and food on the table. I've bought my last pair of Italian shoes, but I was always a deadset K-Mart girl. You could take the kids out for me some weekend. Wonderland, or something.

GERRY: Of course.

ANNIE: And Luke's still football-mad. He's never seen a League game.

GERRY: I'll take him.

ANNIE: Thanks.

Silence.

GERRY: I'm sorry, Annie.

ANNIE: We'll be okay.

◆ ◆ ◆ ◆ ◆

SCENE THIRTY-SIX: 1993

JESSIE *and* THEO *on screen. He is silent.*

JESSIE 28: [*on screen*] They told us we shouldn't try again. We've thought about adopting. But I reckon that energy should maybe go somewhere else. I'm not sure if Theo agrees with me. But that's the way I'm thinking. I like being round kids… but they don't have to be mine.

>*1994.* GERRY *interviews* DOUG *and* ZOE.

GERRY: Last time we talked, Zoe was hoping to go back to school. You haven't done that. Why not?

ZOE: It hasn't worked out that way.

GERRY: Why not?

>*Silence.*

DOUG: We've had to consider our financial situation.

GERRY: Has it changed? How?

ZOE: Turn it off, Gerry.

DOUG: [*to* ZOE] It's all right. [*To* GERRY] Zoe's had to take a part-time job. I've been retrenched. I'm looking for a job.

GERRY: Have you thought about going back to finish your law degree?

ZOE: Yes. If I find full-time work we could manage that.

GERRY: Doug did say he wasn't comfortable about practising law.

>*They glance at each other.*

DOUG: I liked studying law. But once I knew Zoe was pregnant… I felt it was my job to be a provider. The child's needs come first, don't they?

◆ ◆ ◆ ◆ ◆

SCENE THIRTY-SEVEN: 1994

ZOE *and* GERRY *at Susannah's house.*

SUSANNAH: It's a perfect arrangement. Gabrielle loves you.

ZOE: A bit early to say that.

SUSANNAH: Gabrielle's a very choosy girl. She won't let my mother pick her up. But she let you change her.

> *Gabrielle cries offstage.*

That says, I'm hungry. And I want the great tit in the sky.

> *She goes.*

ZOE: Gerry, you're a life-saver. Doug can do his computer course while Sky's at school, then pick her up and help her with her homework. Perfect. She adores him. And he adores her.

GERRY: Why wouldn't he? His own beautiful daughter?

> *Silence.*

ZOE: She wants to learn ballet. Now she can.

GERRY: She's not Doug's child, is she?

ZOE: Do you ever take a day off?

GERRY: She doesn't look anything like him.

ZOE: I don't look anything like my father.

GERRY: She does look like the boy who died. The guitarist.

ZOE: You never met Alex!

GERRY: I went to hear his band at the Zone. Naked Republic. He was a good-looker. Slavic cheekbones, dead ringer for Baryshnikov.

ZOE: Don't do this.

GERRY: This's your private stuff. Until you decide you want to talk about it.

ZOE: If you had a band, it'd be called Thin End of the Wedge.

GERRY: It would be your decision.

ZOE: Is this your fee?

GERRY: My fee?

ZOE: You get me a job, I give you—

GERRY: I don't work like that. I ask questions.

ZOE: Not that question. Doug couldn't take it.

GERRY: Does Sky know? [*Beat.*] She doesn't. Why not?

ZOE: We think she's still too young…

GERRY: We think? Or Doug thinks?

ZOE: Gerry, back off! Sky's father was a heroin user who left me when I told him I was pregnant. He did offer to pay for the abortion. Doug has loved her and cared for her. He has the right to call himself her father.

GERRY: Of course he does. So long as she knows the whole story.

ZOE: Who needs to know the whole story? Only you, Gerry.

◆ ◆ ◆ ◆ ◆

SCENE THIRTY-EIGHT: OUT OF TIME

ROGER *walks in* GERRY*'s dream.*

ROGER: Gerry? Gerry?

GERRY: Roger. Where are you? Where did you go?

ROGER: Will you come for me? You said you'd come when I called.

GERRY: But where did you go?

ROGER: Where you told me to go.

GERRY: Where? Where, Roger?

ROGER: Somewhere far away. Somewhere with nothing. Will you come for me?

GERRY: Where? Tell me where you are. And I'll come.

ROGER: Without a camera?

GERRY: I wouldn't be me without a camera.

◆ ◆ ◆ ◆ ◆

SCENE THIRTY-NINE: GERRY'S HOUSE, 1995

GERRY *stares at a TV screen.* ROGER *is beside him, echoing the* NEWSREADER.

TV NEWSREADER: [*voice-over*] The hills straddle the border of Thailand and Laos, a beautiful but dangerous region that attracts only the most adventurous travellers. Somewhere here the Keren rebels are holding

Chan and his four companions, who were captured outside the Buddhist monastery where they were living. The terrorists say the five will be freed only in exchange for five rebel leaders currently in Chiang Mai jail awaiting execution.

◆ ◆ ◆ ◆ ◆

SCENE FORTY: JESSIE AND THEO'S HOUSE, 1995

JESSIE: No! Whatever's on the tip of your tongue, leave it there.
THEO: Okay. But—
JESSIE: Leave it.
THEO: Okay. Okay. But—
JESSIE: Leave it.
THEO: I'm married to a cause junkie.
JESSIE: We're not married. And this is not a cause. This is about my people.

Kenneth Moraleda (left) as Roger and Steve Bisley as Gerry in the 2002 Sydney Theatre Company production. (Photo: Heidrun Löhr)

THEO: And I can't argue with you, because my mob know nothing about being oppressed and colonised.

JESSIE: Theo—

THEO: One day I'll give you a little rap on the Ottoman Empire. You know how long the Turks occupied Greece?

JESSIE: You kept your culture, you kept your language, you kept your kids. Theo, I'm not going to give you a fucking seminar. It's my life. It's one year in my life. And I'll be on Cape York, not the moon. You can come and visit.

THEO: You know why you're going?

JESSIE: Bub, I need to do it.

THEO: No, Jess. You think you ought to do it. When you were fourteen, someone cast you as a heroine—

JESSIE: No.

THEO: A heroine of his movie.

JESSIE: First time I met you, you quoted it! You loved it!

THEO: I loved *Gallipoli*. But the Turks didn't really shoot at Mel Gibson. That was a movie. Gerry got you up in the Domain, then he took you off to Borneo to save the rain forest. When was that? Twelve, thirteen years ago? Every year since then there's been another cause, another banner, another delegation to Canberra—

JESSIE: This is a community clinic in Weipa! It's my country, the joint's full of Torres Strait people—

THEO: It's still a cause. And you'll be up there on the TV screens of the nation—

JESSIE: No way. I won't tell him.

THEO: Like his girlfriend's going to go bush and he won't know!

JESSIE: His girlfriend? Don't fight dirty.

THEO: I'm fighting for this. For what we have. And we are married, in my mind we are. You're my life. Please don't go.

JESSIE: I'll come back.

THEO: You won't. There'll always be someone else that needs you. You'll give yourself away in big bleeding chunks. And when you wake up and there's none of you left, it'll be too late!

JESSIE: You're talking such shit, Theo. Too late for what?

THEO: I don't know, for the rest of your life!

JESSIE: This is the rest of my life. And here and now, I think it's going nowhere.

THEO: Thanks a fucking heap.

Doorknock.

We're not home.

JESSIE *goes towards it.*

No, Jess. I said no.

JESSIE *goes. She returns with* GERRY.

GERRY: They said there'd be one death for each execution. The Keren rebels have been shooting them in the head and dumping them in the forest. I was there when the fourth body was found.

THEO: Did you get it?

GERRY: Did I get what?

THEO: Did you get it on film?

GERRY: I saw them bringing it in to the village. They'll find Roger eventually.

THEO: Roger's body.

GERRY: Yes, his body. Could I have some coffee?

THEO: You'll want to be there for that, mate.

JESSIE: Bub…

GERRY: I'm a film-maker, Theo. I follow these people's lives.

THEO: All the way home.

JESSIE: Bub!

THEO: That's why he went, isn't it? To see the body brought in.

JESSIE: Theo!

GERRY: Should I be here?

THEO: I'm going to bed.

THEO *goes.*

JESSIE: Sorry. We were in the middle of something.

GERRY: Trouble? [*Beat.*] You can tell me.

She smiles at him and shakes her head.

Talk to me, Jess. I'm in your life.

JESSIE: I'm disappearing, Gerry. For a year. No news. No interview. No questions.

Perhaps ROGER *echoes her last words. She goes.* GERRY *sees* ROGER.

GERRY: I came for you.

ROGER: But you didn't find me. You didn't see me.

On the screen, images of ROGER*'s childhood.* SUSANNAH 7 *sings.*

SUSANNAH: [*singing, voice-over*]
'Au clair de la lune, mon ami Pierrot,
Prête-moi ta plume pour écrire un mot.
Ma chandelle est morte, je n'ai plus de feu.
Ouvre-moi ta porte, pour l'amour de Dieu.'

◆ ◆ ◆ ◆ ◆

SCENE FORTY-ONE: CAM AND ANNIE'S HOUSE, 1995

CAM, *in a wheelchair, with* GERRY.

GERRY: He's a bright boy. He'll say something, and if I close my eyes, it's you.

CAM: He's a lot better educated than I ever was.

GERRY: But no brighter. You were a smart boy.

CAM: Yeah? What happened?

ANNIE *comes in.*

ANNIE: They've had a cracker day. Luke says Gerry's a total legend. Melanie wants you to tuck her in.

CAM: Me or him?

ANNIE: You, Cam.

CAM: Any news of Roger?

GERRY: No news.

CAM *goes.*

I have to run. But before I go, I want to make you an offer.

ANNIE: No, Gerry. I won't sit in front of a camera—

GERRY: That's not it.

ANNIE: And I won't let the kids—

GERRY: Annie, listen. We can make you some money. Real money. Can you say no to that?

ANNIE: Can anyone?

GERRY: I rang round the features editors at the women's magazines, pitched a story.

ANNIE: No way. They were onto us the minute Cam got out of hospital. He wouldn't talk then, and he won't now.

GERRY: Now they want your story.

ANNIE: There's no story. I've been working in a hot bread shop.

GERRY: You've held this family together for three years.

ANNIE: There's no mileage in that.

GERRY: I disagree. So do they. I've jacked them up to twenty-five grand. They'll go higher.

ANNIE: I can't put two words together. I never could, even when—

GERRY: I'll coach you. We might get thirty, thirty-five.

ANNIE: Thirty-five thousand dollars!

GERRY: They will want photos.

ANNIE: He'll never wear it.

GERRY: You can do all the talking. But they'll want you all together in one frame.

ANNIE: You put it to him. It'll sound better, coming from you.

GERRY: No! I'm a silent partner. I'll do you the best deal, and they'll call you to make the arrangements.

ANNIE: You think I can pull this off?

GERRY: Why not? You're strong and you're smart.

ANNIE: I never thought you rated me.

GERRY: Always.

ANNIE: If Cam does agree… I'll have to give you a cut.

GERRY: No, you won't.

ANNIE: I can't keep taking handouts.

GERRY: You can take me out for dinner.

ANNIE: I've got a better idea. We'll go sky-diving. My shout. I'll be thirty in November. We'll take the big jump.

◆ ◆ ◆ ◆ ◆

SCENE FORTY-TWO: 1996

ZOE *at 30 outside a dance-club.*

ZOE 30: [*on screen*] No, Doug doesn't come. He doesn't like clubbing. I come out with a couple of girlfriends. I can't believe I'm thirty. I still feel seventeen. But I know a bit more. Yes, I wanted to educate myself. I thought that meant going back to school. But now I see I can do it on my own, while I'm working. I'm asking more questions. I'm reading more. I'd like to do some more study, some time, but at the moment I'm the breadwinner. But not tonight, hey! Tonight I'm the retro bitch from hell! I'm ready to rage! You want to come in?

◆ ◆ ◆ ◆ ◆

SCENE FORTY-THREE: SUSANNAH'S HOUSE, 1996

ZOE: You're putting words in my mouth. What I meant was—

SUSANNAH: What you said, I heard loud and clear. You said there is something wrong with my child.

GERRY: She said there might be something to be looked at.

SUSANNAH: Something to be looked at. You'd be on board for that, wouldn't you?

ZOE: I didn't dream this up. It's been on my mind for months. She doesn't seem to respond—

SUSANNAH: To you.

ZOE: Or to Gerry.

SUSANNAH: Gerry's been here? While I was at work?

ZOE: He dropped in once or twice.

GERRY: We took Gabrielle to the park. She doesn't seem to notice things outside.

SUSANNAH: She loves her mobile, the Brancusi bird, she loves that. She loves me singing to her. She sees me, she hears me, she responds appropriately. I think we can conclude that her cognitive development is on track.

ZOE: I've read up on this. Sometimes it's hard for the parent to see—

SUSANNAH: Zoe, the day I met you, you were stranded at the gate of the zoo, couldn't put one foot in front of the other. I had to take you by the hand and lead you in. You were hopeless, totally needy.

GERRY: I would have said shy.

SUSANNAH: Needy, always needy. Gabrielle's not needy. She's like me. Exactly like me. She's happy in her own imaginative world.

ZOE: Okay—

SUSANNAH: No, not okay. I'm terminating this arrangement.

ZOE: I've raised this because I was worried.

SUSANNAH: Or because you wanted to make me worried?

GERRY: Why would she want to do that?

SUSANNAH: She might ask herself that question. [*To* ZOE] I'll pay you till the end of the month. Are you two having an affair?

ZOE: No!

SUSANNAH: I saw you. On screen. Out clubbing together.

GERRY: She went clubbing, Susannah. I followed with a camera.

SUSANNAH: And the little daytime visits?

GERRY: I came here because she had some concerns—

SUSANNAH: And who did she turn to? Not me, not the mother. She called the man with the camera.

ZOE: Susannah, how many times have I tried to talk to you? You're too busy to listen, or you listen like I'm stupid.

SUSANNAH: You are. Stupid and vicious. I'll send you a cheque.

> ZOE *goes.*

Isn't it enough that you're enmeshed in our lives? Can't you keep your hands off our children?

GERRY: What do you think I am? The child snatcher out of some fairytale?

SUSANNAH: You're offended! He's offended!

GERRY: It's offensive. And way off the mark. I didn't start this. Zoe told you, she called me.

SUSANNAH: And you dropped everything and ran here to make your snap-frozen judgement on my child. You're not a film-maker, you're an ambulance chaser. Someone else's bad news is your good luck.

GERRY: So you think the news might be bad?

SUSANNAH: This is about you, not Gabrielle. You've found your genre, and it's not documentary, it's disaster movies. You tell Roger to go and find himself, and he loses his life. You go on the town with Cam and he slams into a wall and cripples himself. What have you got planned for Jessie? Death in custody? No, it's the boys that string themselves up—

GERRY: Susannah, get a grip on yourself!

SUSANNAH: And Jessie can't crash. Jessie's the star of this show. She'll be the last one standing.

GERRY: There is something wrong with Gabrielle. And you know it, better than any of us. You work with kids all day, every day, at Westmead, you're smart and perceptive. You're a watcher, you see and you know.

SUSANNAH: I don't want to know you. I don't want to see you again. I don't want to hear from you. I wish I'd never met you.

◆ ◆ ◆ ◆ ◆

SCENE FORTY-FOUR: SUBURBAN BALLET SCHOOL, 1997

Ballet music. On screen, a suggestion of a ballet class. GERRY *shoots the unseen sky.* DOUG *approaches with an Instamatic camera.*

GERRY: She's putting everything into it.

DOUG: We've never pushed her. She loves it.

GERRY: And the camera loves her.

DOUG: Do you think a camera can love?

GERRY: It likes good bone structure. And hers is pretty fine.

DOUG: Zoe was right. You have X-ray eyes. She gets her bones from her father. Her birth father. Maybe the dancing, too.

GERRY: Does she know about him?

DOUG: She knows she's had two fathers, and I'm the one that chose to stay. We were honest. Now we're even closer as a family.

ZOE *approaches.*

Why didn't you tell us you'd be here?

GERRY: I did tell Zoe. I said I'll cut you a home movie. Didn't I?

ZOE: It'll be a nice Christmas present for your parents. Their own little ballerina.

DOUG: We could have discussed this at home.

ZOE: I forgot to mention it.

DOUG: Funny thing to forget.

ZOE: Yes.

Music starts.

She's off. I've got to turn her into a sugar plum.

ZOE *goes.* GERRY *is following.*

DOUG: You're not to talk to Sky. You hear me?

GERRY: She talked to me before. Remember? Showed me her secret document box. You liked that.

DOUG: We had a real secret then, and I thought it was safe.

GERRY: It is.

DOUG: I've watched you at work.

GERRY: And you've watched the results every year for how long? Ten, twelve years? You never see me. I never narrate, I never comment. How could a secret come out? Only through you, through Zoe—

DOUG: Through Sky. And now you know what she… Look, you've already nailed me as a loser—

GERRY: No way.

DOUG: The perennial job-seeker, the house-husband making the casserole, the dad waiting with the mums at the school gates, I can wear all that. But to have strangers know that I'm doing it for a child that isn't mine—

GERRY: That makes you a good man.

DOUG: That makes me a good story. And you'll keep working till you get it. But I won't let you. This story's closed. No more Doug, no more Zoe, no more Sky. See, we're not three separate lives, we're a unit. You mightn't understand that.

GERRY: This is my life's work. You mightn't understand that.

DOUG: I don't have a life's work? That's what you think, at least that's how you show me. My life's work is my family. And from here on, this will do us. Family snaps.

◆ ◆ ◆ ◆ ◆

SCENE FORTY-FIVE: 1998

JESSIE 32 *at Weipa.*

JESSIE 32: [*on screen*] No, I wasn't meant to stay. Like you weren't meant to turn up here. I was here for one year. But we were trying to do some things here, and we hadn't got them done, and I thought all it needed was a bit more effort, and a bit more time… Theo came up for a month. That was nice, but he got restless. He needs his soccer and his sourdough bread and his coffee. He's a city boy. I thought I was a city girl, but when I went back last Christmas, this place was in my dreams. Up here, I never dream about the city. I like this mob. I get the shits once a week, I have a run-in with ATSIC or Telstra or somebody, and I say I'm out of here. It'll be time to leave soon enough. I miss Theo. I miss my family. I'll come back soon.

◆ ◆ ◆ ◆ ◆

SCENE FORTY-SIX: OUT OF TIME

ROGER *walks in* GERRY*'s dream.*

GERRY: I came for you.
ROGER: But you didn't find me. You didn't see me.
GERRY: I see you now. I don't know why. Tell me why I'm seeing you?
ROGER: You'll work it out. You always do.
GERRY: When?
ROGER: When you finish it.

GERRY: But I can't. You're gone. Zoe's out. Susannah's out. Cam won't talk. How do I finish it?

ROGER: You'll find a way. It's your life's work.

◆ ◆ ◆ ◆ ◆

SCENE FORTY-SEVEN: CAM AND ANNIE'S BACKYARD, 1998

GERRY *is with* ANNIE, *drinking.*

GERRY: I will finish it. They want it to go to air on the first of January 2000. And I will deliver. Somehow.

ANNIE: Gerry? Can we talk?

GERRY: You know it will be hard.

ANNIE: To talk?

GERRY: To finish. To get close to Susannah again—

ANNIE: We need to talk.

GERRY: To get to Zoe, which means getting past Doug. To get Cam to talk, how do I do that?

ANNIE: Gerry—

GERRY: Jessie. She's the key. Don't you reckon? Jessie. Good old Jessie.

ANNIE: Good old Jessie.

GERRY: She's the centre. She'll be home soon. And I've always got you.

ANNIE: Good old Annie.

GERRY: Sorry. I've been raving. Talk to me.

ANNIE: Gerry, this is not... I don't feel great about this...

> *He embraces her. The embrace turns passionate. She pulls away.*

No, Gerry.

GERRY: Please.

ANNIE: No. I can't do this any more.

GERRY: Why did you call me?

ANNIE: To talk.

GERRY: We talk. Don't we?

ANNIE: No, mate. We eat, we have sex and you drive me home. Tonight I am home. Cam and the kids are inside. You'd better go.

GERRY: No.

ANNIE: Go home. This is not… it's not right.

GERRY: It's honest. You don't love me, I don't love you. But we like each other, and we still want each other. Don't we? I want you, Annie…

ANNIE: All right. But never again.

> CAM *is watching.*

CAM: Never again. Is that the big turn-on every time?

> *Silence.*

ANNIE: How long have you known?

CAM: Depends what you mean by known…

ANNIE: This only started a few months ago.

CAM: He's been cruising you for years, ever since—

GERRY: Bullshit.

CAM: No, mate. Truth.

ANNIE: Say what you like to me, Cam. But don't pay out on him. He's kept us afloat for six years—

GERRY: Annie.

ANNIE: He's been a father to your kids—

GERRY: Let's stop this. Let's say we're sorry, and—

CAM: He's done it all. Show him how grateful you are. Do him right here and I'll shoot.

GERRY: Cut it out, Cam.

CAM: Great little action sequence to wrap up our story.

GERRY: Cam, I'm sorry.

CAM: But our story already got wrapped up, didn't it, mate?

GERRY: I said I'm sorry.

CAM: You going to be featuring that in the year 2000?

GERRY: Cam, please…

ANNIE: Featuring what?

GERRY: We didn't know what we were doing, either of us.

CAM: You knew.

ANNIE: What's he talking about? Tell me, Gerry.

GERRY: Believe me, you don't want to know.

CAM: He doesn't want you to know. But it's the greatest scene he never showed. A mighty action sequence. A man spinning out.

GERRY: No, please—

ANNIE: Who's this man? One of you? Which one?

CAM: Depends on where you were sitting. I was the one at the wheel. He was the one with the camera.

ANNIE: [*to* GERRY] You shot him while he was driving? You asked him questions? Did you let it happen? Or… did you make it happen?

> *We are in* GERRY*'s head. Only he hears the remembered conversation,* CAM*'s last words before the crash. Perhaps* CAM *is out of the wheelchair now, or else* GERRY *hears…*

CAM 26: [*voice-over*] The big men used to tell me, it's like they'd done a deal with the devil. First they make you famous, then they make you pay for it. And I'd tell them I'll never pay for anything. But tonight it hit me. I did a deal with the devil. And it's you. You're the devil. We did our deal and now I'm paying for it. And I'll keep paying, won't I? Won't I, Gerry? Body and soul.

> *Abruptly come the sound and image of the crash.*

◆ ◆ ◆ ◆ ◆

SCENE FORTY-EIGHT:
THEO AND JESSIE'S BACKYARD, 26 JANUARY 2000

THEO *arranges food and drink.* JESSIE *brings incense sticks and a candle.*

THEO: You should have a hat.

JESSIE: I'll get it.

THEO: In this heat you should have a hat.

> ROGER *is there, sitting quietly.* THEO *cannot see him.* JESSIE *may see or at least sense him.*

JESSIE: He's here.

THEO: Who?

JESSIE: Roger. He's here.

THEO: I hope so. It's his party.

> ZOE *and* DOUG *arrive.*

ZOE: Jess, you should have a hat.

THEO: See?

JESSIE: I'll get one.

> *She gives the candle to* ZOE *and goes inside.*

DOUG: She looks good.

THEO: She says Roger's here.

ZOE: I'm glad she remembered. It's good to remember.

> SUSANNAH *enters the yard.*

THEO: Hi. Susannah. I'm Theo.

SUSANNAH: Of course you're Theo. Perfect day for this. Hello, Doug. Zoe. How's Sky?

DOUG: She's terrific.

ZOE: Hormonal but terrific. Going into Year Nine. How's Gabrielle?

SUSANNAH: Terrific. She's at a holiday camp. She's swimming now. And she paints, all the time. Beautiful fish, beautiful birds…

ZOE: I'd like to see her again.

> JESSIE *comes out with* CAM *and* ANNIE. *She now wears a hat. General greetings.*

ANNIE: We've got a good day for it. Happy new millennium.

JESSIE: The year we turn thirty-five. Roger was first. He had the easiest birthday to remember.

ROGER: I'm Australian, same as you. I was born on Australia Day.

THEO: Invasion Day.

JESSIE: Survival Day. Today.

> *Only* JESSIE *sees* GERRY *arrive.*

He was taken today. Five years ago.

THEO: Jess says he's here today.

JESSIE: He is if we're all here to remember him.

ZOE: Are we all here?

> GERRY *enters. They all turn to see him.*

GERRY: Jess and Theo asked me. And I came for Roger.

ROGER: You didn't see me. You didn't find me.

GERRY: I came for Roger.

SUSANNAH: Of course.

> SUSANNAH *shakes his hand, not warmly.* ZOE *and* JESSIE *kiss him,* THEO *and* DOUG *shake his hand.* CAM *acknowledges him.* ANNIE *kisses him, briefly.* JESSIE *is lighting incense.*

JESSIE: There's a little Buddha there. If you'd like to plant a stick of incense—

SUSANNAH: Roger's family was Anglican.

JESSIE: He spent his last year as a Buddhist. So if you want to do that…

GERRY: I'd be really grateful if I could stay. With the camera.

SUSANNAH: Why?

ROGER: You know why.

SUSANNAH: It's over. Isn't it? Years ago.

GERRY: The network wanted to wrap it up on New Year's Day. I asked them to wait till you'd all got to thirty-five.

From left: Justine Clarke as Annie, Travis McMahon as Cam, Anthony Weigh as Doug, Kate Mulvany as Zoe and Steve Bisley as Gerry in the 2002 Sydney Theatre Company production. (Photo: Heidrun Löhr)

ANNIE: But who's still in?

GERRY: I've got enough to make some statement about all of you. It would be good to have some closure. But that's up to you. At least today we can honour Roger. Can I shoot this?

> *Silence.*

Any objections?

> *All shrug or shake their heads.*

SUSANNAH: But I won't talk. Not today. Not ever.

GERRY: Even if you could say whatever you like? Wrap it up in your own way?

SUSANNAH: I have wrapped it up.

DOUG: We're no longer a part of this.

ANNIE: Cam and me… likewise.

THEO: And I think we'd find it hard to… continue. Wouldn't we, Jess?

ROGER: Today will be the end.

GERRY: Today will be the end.

JESSIE: Not for me. I'm beginning something tomorrow.

THEO: Jess…

JESSIE: A course of chemo. I'm the last birthday. I'm December. I plan to be here for that.

THEO: You will be.

JESSIE: It'll be a big year for Theo and me. And if Gerry needs to be there, I'm happy.

> *All are still, looking at* JESSIE *as she moves among them, passing out incense sticks. On screen, the little Buddha with the burning sticks. All stay as* ROGER *moves around the group, touching* SUSANNAH, ZOE *and* CAM. GERRY *begins to shoot.* ROGER *takes* JESSIE*'s hand and leads her away. As they leave we see on the screen some images of* JESSIE*'s death in hospital.*

JESSIE 14: [*voice-over*] I want time to be all the things that I can be. None of us want that time taken from us. We want our chance at life.

◆ ◆ ◆ ◆ ◆

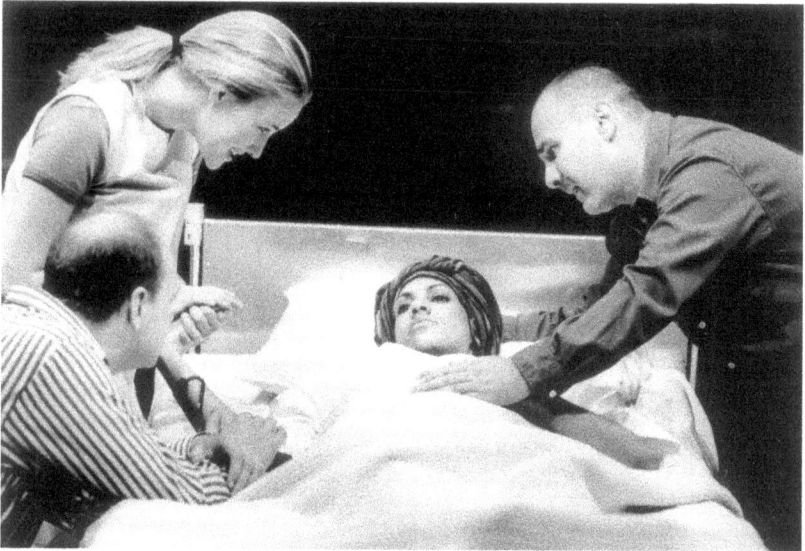

Clockwise from top left: Kate Mulvany as Zoe, Arky Michael as Theo,
Margaret Harvey as Jessie and Anthony Weigh as Doug in the 2002
Sydney Theatre Company production. (Photo: Heidrun Löhr)

SCENE FORTY-NINE:
A WEEK LATER, AN OPEN SPACE NEAR WATER, 2000

SUSANNAH, CAM *and* ANNIE, DOUG *wait.* ZOE *and* THEO *come to meet them.*

ZOE: This way. Her family are all out on the headland.

THEO: We've got a good day for it. Let's go.

>   *He sees* GERRY *approaching with his camera.*

No way. No way, pal.

GERRY: I'll keep my distance. This is hard on you, mate. But today is the
end of something.

THEO: Thanks. Now we've got that clear—

ZOE: Theo, let it go.

THEO: I need to get something else clear. Will you show what you shot
in the hospital?

GERRY: Jessie was happy for me to—

THEO: She wanted to make you happy. So you took her last moment. You took her death from me, and you took it from yourself. You could have been there.

GERRY: I was there.

THEO: You could have been with her. With us. You kept your distance. Keep your distance today.

ZOE: No, Theo.

SUSANNAH: Let him come without his camera.

THEO: Too late. He's got us all. He got her, right to the end.

CAM: Let him come, mate.

THEO: If he destroys everything he shot in the hospital. Can you throw it all away?

> ROGER *has joined the group.* GERRY *sees him.*

ROGER: Can you?

GERRY: No.

THEO: You'll use it?

GERRY: Yes.

THEO: Please don't join us. [*He turns to the others.*] Her family are waiting.

> THEO *walks towards the headland.* ZOE, DOUG, SUSANNAH *and* ANNIE *and* CAM *follow.* JESSIE *leaves.* GERRY *is left alone with* ROGER.

GERRY: What do I do?

ROGER: Finish it.

GERRY: Finish it. How?

> ROGER *takes the camera. He turns it on* GERRY. *Suddenly we see, for the first time on screen,* GERRY*'s face. He turns to see himself.* ROGER *keeps filming.* GERRY*'s face fills the screen.*

No! No!

> *He tries to move out of the frame.* ROGER *keeps the camera trained on him.*

ROGER: Begin.

GERRY: No.

ROGER: Begin. I want your child.

GERRY: I want your child.

ROGER: What do I want from them?

GERRY: What do I want from them? One day out of their lives. One day a year…

ROGER: Till…

GERRY: Till they turn… Till they die.

On the screen, he sees JESSIE*'s last moments.*

One day for the camera to follow them. To a football game, a ballet class, a birthday party, whatever. One day a year for them to speak and be heard. I'd like to be in their lives. Yes, I'd like to be in their lives. No, I'd like them to be in my life. I'd like them to be my life.

He is mumbling now.

I'd like them to live for me.

ROGER: What?

GERRY: I'd like them to live for me.

GERRY *is seven years old now.*

THE FIVE CHILDREN: [*severally*] I know what you're going to do. You talk to us. Then you do it again next year. And you'll put the two films together and see how we've changed. And then the next year, you'll do the same thing. But why?

THE END

Steve Bisley as Gerry in the 2002 Sydney Theatre Company production.
(Photo: Heidrun Löhr)

www.ingramcontent.com/pod-product-compliance
Lightning Source LLC
Chambersburg PA
CBHW041932090426

42744CB00017B/2020